My Luck in the
Blind Girl

Iyke Odiche Ozoma

My Luck in the Blind Girl by Iyke Odiche Ozoma

ISBN 978-1-970072-74-7 (Paperback)
ISBN 978-1-970072-75-4 (Hardback)

This book is written to provide information and motivation to readers. Its purpose is not to render any type of psychological, legal, or professional advice of any kind. The content is the sole opinion and expression of the author, and not necessarily that of the publisher.

Copyright © 2019 by Iyke Odiche Ozoma

All rights reserved. No part of this book may be reproduced, transmitted, or distributed in any form by any means, including, but not limited to, recording, photocopying, or taking screenshots of parts of the book, without prior written permission from the author or the publisher. Brief quotations for noncommercial purposes, such as book reviews, permitted by Fair Use of the U.S. Copyright Law, are allowed without written permissions, as long as such quotations do not cause damage to the book's commercial value. For permissions, write to the publisher, whose address is stated below.

Printed in the United States of America.

New Leaf Media, LLC
175 S. 3rd Street, Suite 200
Columbus, OH 43215
www.thenewleafmedia.com

Contents

Chapter 1: Adanne, the Blind Girl 1

Chapter 2: Adanne on the Campus 38

Chapter 3: The Jinx Broken 60

Chapter 4: The Conglomeration 92

About the author 141

About the book 143

Chapter One

Adanne, the Blind Girl

Adanne was born like every other "normal" being, without any encroaching disabilities. Her birth was as perfect as possible. She was a child born surging with the prospect of representing God's favor.

She was born physically healthy and mentally sound. In fact, she came as a favor, a door opener for the family of Mr. Udenwa, whose beautiful wife had been barren for over four years following their marriage.

The celebration of such a birth would have hit the heights of heaven if not for the family's lack of money. But that lack did not completely succeed in taking away the joy that visited the family. Mr. Udenwa tried his very best to show his appreciation to God.

Adanne started growing, without the spots of illnesses every other baby experienced. Her future seemed promising. There was hope that she would be a pride and solace to her family. She was beautiful, respectful, intelligent, and brilliant. Though pampered, she was not spoilt; Adanne did not allow the high level of affection showered on her by her parents to go to her head. She maintained sobriety, as she was taught discipline from the womb.

At the age of thirteen, she was already finishing her primary education, rare in the remote village where she lived during the postcolonial era. She showed high levels of self-dependency in all her academic work. The same was true even in her farmwork.

Adanne could do what other children of her age could not do in the domestic sphere of the family. Adanne was able to stand in for her mother when her mother was not around.

At school, she was also very good at physical exercise that required the use of her hands. She endeared herself to the head teacher and other teachers, garnering their unfeigned admiration. They had her lead everything the school did.

Because of her good academic showing, Adanne could not help but sink herself into her academic interests. She vowed to herself and to her family that she would not disappoint them in her pursuit of an education. She would be a source of pride for them. It was a promise that did not need to be voiced in order to be fully comprehended.

Adanne carried out this vision without missing a step. Though her parents were not rich, they were capable of providing for her academic needs. Even though feeding the family was a major effort, Adanne's academic needs suffered no stress.

Adanne was the good girl in the small village of farmers and peasant traders. This attribute came from her self-controlled conduct, which was based on a high dependency on Christianity. She never argued with the demand of obedience to both natural and human righteousness. She never missed any program or service at the Catholic Church to which she belonged. And she fully believed the creed. Out of habit, she made sure to finish her domestic chores on time to attend the program in the thatched-roof church as a member of the Bible study society.

She conducted prayers during the prayer meetings and taught the Bible when needed. Adanne handled the prayer meetings with a renewed mind towards salvation and blessings from God. The skill with which she handled her class made members try to attend every day she taught.

Adanne's parents were so proud of her—not in conceit but in an acknowledgement of the blessings she brought to the family. This made her a yardstick with which other parents measured their daughters, especially those close to her age.

The good remarks Adanne received did not go down well with every girl; some felt jealousy and hatred towards her. Adanne was well aware of this and did not attempt to retaliate. Instead, she offered the other girls genuine love, and she welcomed and accommodated them with open arms when they sought her assistance with their academic shortcomings or challenges.

Adanne was a jewel to emulate. Serious-minded individuals scrambled to repeat her script of life and see how it would bless their lives. Those whose lives revolved around waywardness benefited from the rare gem in her, yet they still reviled the way she led her life.

But Adanne paid no attention. She was occupied with how to satisfy her parents and help stamp out the endemic poverty that ravaged them. This was the stone upon which they stood to find reasons to mock her.

It was Adanne's life led based on high self-worth that brought her the admiration of the village. It gave her the grace necessary to loathe any negative advances and not abuse the trust and love she enjoyed from her parents, the villagers, and the school authority. Even teachers from neighboring villages sang her praises to admonish their students beyond Adanne's reach.

She avoided folklore, which contained in it self-deceit. She saw it as a trap too deadly to risk. She comfortably lived in her isolated dream of a hopeful future.

***

One day, the devil struck. Adanne lost everything when the devil visited, as though working for those who could not condone her well-rated conduct. One fateful day, Adanne and other pupils were going to the neighboring village to work on the farm of one of their teachers. That was the school routine on Thursdays, called "Labor Day."

The hours between 11:00 a.m. and 1:30 p.m. on Thursdays were dedicated to physical work for the pupils as a part of their practical agricultural science class. They would either work in the school farm, called the garden, or they were taken to their teachers' farms to work. In addition, some of the pupils voluntarily fetched water for their teachers after school or on weekends.

On one of those Thursdays, Adanne met a situation that negatively transformed her life. In just a few seconds, her vision and aspirations diminished. And a new life of agony began for the former jewel of the town on whom high, towering hopes—not only for her but also for the entire village—were built.

Adanne's teacher, who was from the neighboring village, loved how Adanne led her life of goodness—a path that she hoped all would emulate and that brought hope for the future. On this particular Thursday, as earlier announced by the teacher, the pupils went to her village to work on her farm. Nobody objected because the teacher was good to the class. She treated and encouraged the children as if they were hers, perhaps because she was barren and in her early forties, with over ten years of marriage.

The pupils joyfully left the classroom and, carrying their farm implements, headed to Otoko village. As usual, Adanne was in the lead because she was not known to be lackadaisical in anything she did. She showed zeal for everything she was involved in and approached an activity as if her whole life depended on it. Her attitude stirred love in those around her each time she displayed it.

Adanne was now about thirteen years old, and she had sat for the entrance examination for secondary school. Considering her brilliance and academic history, the result was foreknown. She had started preparing for enrolment, considering the fact that she would surely pass. But she expected to be frustrated by the financial aspect of secondary school. Her parents, considering their sorry financial state, had rallied around her, working hard and even borrowing to have the money in time for registration, so she would not lose her opportunity.

The pupils marched on in the small thick bush, like soldiers on the warpath, heading to the teacher's farmland and carrying their farm implements, which clearly made them look like a rampaging group of agitators. A big cobra, hiding in the bush saw them approach. It sensed the pupils' marching as that of angry youths coming to attack it. Seeing the farm implements they carried justified the cobra's assumption. It hid in a corner, watching as they drew closer.

The pupils, unaware of a watching devil laying siege against them, marched on, with Adanne in the lead, meters ahead of the rest. She walked along with the teacher. As she neared the snake, it arose and grew tall, poised to attack. Before Adanne saw the snake, and when she had no possible escape route, the cobra attacked her, releasing its venom into her eyes. Unfortunately, the cobra slithered away immediately. The other pupils and the teacher, who couldn't run very well, retreated, shouting and scaling fences.

Adanne fell to the ground, crying loudly for help. But the others had run back to the main road. The pupils somersaulted over each other while retreating. The teacher fell into a pit and dislocated her ankle. She shouted for help. But just as the pupils had been so scared they could not help Adanne, they continued running for their dear lives, abandoning their teacher as well.

As the students shouted for help, running to the main road, some able-bodied men working in the bush and some passers-by ran to their rescue. They were hardly able to get out the words to tell those who came to help that Adanne was trapped in the bush. But as the rescuers heard the word *snake* and then made out Adanne's pity-arousing cry for help, they ran in the direction her cry was coming from.

Coming upon the teacher trapped in a pit, they tried to rescue her. At first, they thought she was the one who had been shouting for help. But then they heard the cries again. They heard in the caller's voice that she was in excruciating pain. As they ran to meet Adanne, one boy carried her to the road while the others searched for the snake so they could kill it.

Adanne's cries were disturbing. "My eyes!" she shouted. "My school!"

Meanwhile, the boys frantically searched for the snake in all the nooks and crannies of the bushes. They combed the bush with anger, prepared to descend on the snake, given the great damage it had done to the eyes and future of the beautiful girl. But they could not find it anywhere.

Adanne's cries were like a bitter dirge that attracted everybody. Even the villagers who did not know her came, wondering what kind of girl this beautiful lamenting girl could be. Her mates joined her in wails that surpassed those of a young widow watching her beloved husband lowered to the earth. Nothing seemed to be working out.

The most dangerous situation was that the snake would not be found and killed, rendering the villagers unable Tim cook the snake so that Adanne could eat a piece of its meat. If that happened, she would definitely not see again. This was the traditional belief of the people. And they knew the remedy really worked, as it had been used on some victims in the region in the past.

The more Adanne remembered this, the more she cried her heart out. She pleaded passionately for those around her to go after the snake. They all truly poured out their strength to locate and kill the snake but to no avail. Adanne rolled on the ground, crying profusely. Her mates cried for her without touching her, out of the fear of the possible blindness in store for her. The young men exhausted their strength looking for the devil.

Soon, the sad news, which travels faster than good news, reached her people. They flew down to the scene to see for themselves this most incredible story. As they made their way to the scene, their imaginations went wild, their mind traversing all possibilities.

By the time they arrived, Adanne had already been brought out of the bush to the main road. Although the search party had intensified its efforts to locate and kill the snake, none among them had recorded the slightest success. The ramification of the failure was the increasing danger of Adanne becoming blind.

Adanne's mother held her, dropping to the ground before even getting the full details of the incident and wailing like a child. She cried like a child receiving an injection from the nurse. One could not determine if it was the mother or the child who was crying the most.

When Adanne saw that her mother was there, she shouted over and over again, "Mother! They have killed your beloved daughter. Mother! I have been made blind. My hopes, our hopes have been destroyed. I have been made blind, Mother!"

As her daughter's cries attacked her soul, Adanne's mother became so laden with emotion that she fainted momentarily.

The more the mother heard her lamentation, the more she felt she was being crushed mercilessly. She hardly even held Adanne but, rather, lay on the side of the road, crying and rolling on the ground. The younger siblings, who had ran to the scene alongside their mother, only patted Adanne, consoling her and telling her to stop crying. They were more or less unaware of what was happening and the magnitude of the situation at hand.

As for Mazi Udenwa, he merely walked from one side of the road to the other aimlessly, ranting in a violent state and claiming that somebody had done this to his daughter.

He shouted furiously, saying that those who had been jealous of his daughter's brightness had succeeded in putting an end to the glories of God manifesting in her. His words bewildered the villagers of Otoko, where the incident had taken place, who had joined in the rescue mission. They were quite ignorant of what went on in the neighboring village.

Some of them stood speechless as they watched Mazi Udenwa cry like a baby, refusing to let anyone hold him. Others tried to pacify him, telling him to pray that the snake be found and killed so that his daughter would see again and saying that it was not the time to start apportioning blame. But Mazi would reply that they could not understand and that "they" had finally ensured the extinction of his linage.

Some of his kinsmen, who had followed him to the scene on hearing Adanne's ordeal, explained that he was like a man being drowned. They said that he could say anything and that, if it were another person, he would act the same. As such, they concentrated on how to search out the snake and kill it, without which Mazi's daughter would not see again. This was the feeling that ravaged the father, like a missile in his head.

Even if Mazi mentioned names, nobody would take him seriously, considering the magnitude of pain that was ravaging his heart at that very moment. Even they themselves were in pain due to the child's predicament; they couldn't imagine what her biological parents were enduring. And as such, they understood and tolerated him.

Adanne was now carried home on a bicycle, supported by two able-bodied men, to begin a new journey of a changed life. It was a journey of life from prospects to peril, from smiles to sorrows, and from greatness to gnashing of teeth. She went from a life lived in grace to a life in the grass. Adanne's destiny has been rewritten, not for good but for sorrow with no end. A bright star had turned into a dull rock .

For a very long time of many months, Adanne never sheathed the sword that was her tongue. She cried and cursed the day of her birth. She was emaciated as a result of malnutrition. She frequently refused to eat, despite many attempts of pacification, coupled with unfounded promises of coming hope.

The trouble that befell the family was not really Adanne's sudden predicament but her refusal to accept the situation as it was and move forward. But forward to where? She had no forward to move onto. Rather, she saw in her future only retardation to the worst, having not only lost her cherished life ambition—education—but also having been relegated to blindness by the same nature that had been so inimical to the rest of her family from the onset of the world.

Adanne became so emotionally beaten that she forgot her Almighty God—the God she had once been ready to fight for, standing up to anybody blaspheming Him before her. The very same God she had once defended with her last breath, she now denigrated with her whole being as an untrustworthy being.

No amount of encouragement gave meaning to her. She did not see how a blind girl could suddenly become someone useful. Worse was the perennial state of the family's poor financial showing, which she had sworn to bring to its knees. Now, it would enslave her family even more. She was choked by the anger her ordeal brought to her.

Her mother, her beloved friend of no comparison, who she never disobeyed, and her lovely father, who she revered despite his poverty after Christ, now became clowns to listen to. Despite their assurances that they would take good care of her, she rebuffed all their promises and raged like a wounded lioness—wounded not by lions but by lambs.

MY LUCK IN THE BLIND GIRL

Having lost her beautiful physique to the injurious pains, she now looked like a shadow of herself. She was disgusting and demeaning in appearance now. Each time she left her daughter's side or heard her grumble, Adanne's mother could not help but bury herself in tears, though she tried to keep Adanne from seeing her weeping.

But Oriaku Nwayimma could not go far from her. She was always around, soothing her. She was around so much, in fact, that she, for the most part, failed to attend to her trade of vegetable sales or going to the farm. This situation also affected her emotionally, along with the family's welfare, which partly depended on her daily meager gains.

When she went out, she would always hurry back to soothe Adanne. Given the way her daughter was handling the tragedy that had befallen her, she presumed that, if she was left unattended for a long time, Adanne might resort to harming herself. Hence, she stayed close always, safeguarding her from any other harm, since she could no longer see.

Though Adanne had begun to listen to her mother, who would always hold her in her arms and soothe her, she would sometimes flare up again; she would speak the vilest words her mouth could utter. Though she would pretend to be calm at times, in order to give her mother peace, otherwise she only burned inwardly. She could not succeed in putting paid to the issue.

Though she was beginning to come to terms with the situation, she could not stop crying and pleading with her father to search for the snake and kill it so that she might see again. She would cry at the top of her lungs, and her father would assure her that he would kill the snake.

Mazi Udenwa was not lying when he made his promise to Adanne that he would ensure the snake was killed so that she might see again. But the truth was that Mazi had reached his limit. He had tried everything within his ability, to the point of borrowing money so that he could pay a search party in Otoko village, where the incident had taken place, and another one from his village to unravel the hidden place of the snake. But the parties had reached the bounds of their ability to do anything. Yet they could not find the snake, which invariably meant that Adanne would remain blind.

Still, Adanne was not convinced. She accused her father of insensitivity to her plight. This saddened Mazi Ude, who had gone beyond his limit to solve this mystery. He had exhausted his strength trying to discover the hiding snake. Meanwhile Adanne continued to rage, accusing her parents of lacking seriousness about the whole issue. She felt deeply that she had been abandoned, as she was unable to witness the tireless efforts that her father had already poured into helping her.

Adanne's disturbance became quite worrisome, making the family very uncomfortable. Her constant cries, this time for her father to get the snake and kill it, were something no one would like to experience. It simply seemed as if Adanne had lost her sanity, judging from the way she put forward her unattainable requests—all that she may be able to see again.

The truth was that she is angry at everything that she could remember, mostly her aborted ambition. Her worries wore everybody out. Her mother only came around because of the mother-child bond that could hardly be affected by emotions. Yet the situation was never easy for anyone to tolerate without inward grumblings, as restful sleep had been stolen from the family, a victim of Adanne's plight.

At one point in time, the whole thing became uneasy for her father. He could not rest from Adanne's troubles both day and night. Apart from the emotional trauma he had suffered, his anger had flared up at her, and he was losing the love he had for her. He could no longer refrain and, instead, poured out his undiluted anger. He openly criticized her for her continued disturbances despite all efforts to make her see reason and endure.

"It is high time you started accepting your fate," Mazi told his daughter. "What is all this? Did we cause it? You can bear witness that we never faltered in our love towards you. We have always done everything we could to give you a future, matching the diligence you showed. But today, the story is different. In as much as we share in your pains, we cannot kill ourselves. Why do you want all of us to go through the same trauma, Adanne? If it were possible, I would give you my eyes and have yours, but it is not. Why don't you understand for once? Did we send you to Otoko? Do I have a farmland there?"

"It's OK, Nnayi. That's enough. You are being too harsh on her. Can you imagine what she's going through? You know how it feels. Talk more of her who endures the ravaging pain. It tells more of the real victim. Nnayi, please. I can feel your pain. But please calm down," Nwayimma said politely before turning to cuddle Adanne and murmuring that she should not mind her father.

Adanne cried uncontrollably, saying, "Is this not my beloved father talking to me this way in my condition? Does he know what I go through? If I had been born blind, it would have been better for me. Having seen nothing, having no ambition—that would have been better. But to live and die as useless as I came into this world."

"It's okay!" her mother advised her.

She laid her head on the shoulders of her mother and sobbed while soliloquizing her pains. Meanwhile, her father jumped on his bicycle and rode away, ranting in anger as though he waited for such opportunity to explode and pour out his mind.

When her mother left, going into the hut to do some chores, Adanne relaxed and meditated on her father's statement. She saw reasons in his words. She would have to accept her fate—the fate that has changed her life. Though she found the words of reproof encouraging, she nonetheless berated her father for not understanding her plight, which engulfed her and caused her excruciating pain. She asked God questions with no answers.

The one thing Adanne could not forget was the statement her father had made that, "after all, you are not the only child in the house". This she saw as clear abandonment and a sign that he wasn't serious about the discovery of the snake, just as she had assumed.

Each time the statement flashed through her mind, she would lose her spiritual quietude even as(she has stopped much of her crying and disturbance). She felt that her father had changed along with her circumstances. She recalled that he had told her, "You cannot stop the welfare of others." And he had said that he would also take care of "those whose welfare have been affected by your troubles."

Adanne, on hearing this in her mind repeatedly, recoiled and inwardly forgave her father. She also reconciled herself with her present condition and moved on. She stopped crying, grumbling, or reproving anybody. She realized that her present unacceptable state had not been masterminded by any of her family members and wondered why she had found them culpable.

She then spoke in confidence to her mother about the fact that she had accepted her fate and moved on. She would shed the sensitivity that had been partially glued to her soul. She still soliloquized sometimes, without allowing anybody to feel that she was grumbling over the issue. She had promised her mother that she'd given up the worries and moved on.

Adanne's present state impressed her mother very much. As always, she communicated what was going on with Adanne's to the father who had already lost interest in her, though, and was not willing to hear anything about her again, given that she had accused him of orchestrating her plight. But his wife pleaded with him to see reason. She urged him to see all that had taken place from Adanne's point of view—her loss of ambition and the way her joy in life had been suppressed.

But Mazi Udenwa never offered anybody any reconciliation. Instead he also raged. He lamented the amount he had wasted hiring search parties to look for the snake. Yet Adanne had still accused him of insensitivity.

Adanne went to her father and asked his forgiveness. She also asked him to take care of the others, who the Lord had showered with blessings, and to forget her in her irreparable state, leaving her to live and die.

She sympathized with her siblings, whose future had been scarred by her predicament. They had stopped going to school because their school fees had also been used to pay for the search parties from Otoko village and their own village.

She felt for them. Even with the situation, they had never showed her antipathy but had always stayed by her, patting her back and saying they were "sorry" whenever she flared up.

Consequently, a truce was reached. Adanne's submission to her fate had calmed the storm a bit. Nonetheless, Adanne still felt unhappy inwardly, even though she tried her level best to hide it. She became temperamental and very erratic.

Adanne's erratic behavior continued, but she did not cry again. Neither did she disturb her family or accuse anybody of treating her badly. One good part about the trend in her changing mood was that she never agreed to give up her desire to be somebody in life, despite her disability.

Thus her desire for improvement in her life situation despite her unaccepted disability sparked off another round of problems in her family. She began to plead with her parents again, this time asking them to get her glasses so that she might resume her studies.

This demand resuscitated the buried tension of Adanne's disturbance in the house, as she never ceased for a moment crying for glasses. The situation once again bored into the entire family, who had believed that Adanne's troublemaking was over. The idea particularly, stung her father who saw it as a pure waste of money.

Her father, with his anger and restive temperament, unleashed and attack on Adanne when her demands next resurfaced. He dismissed the idea as an inconsequential, considering the fact that she has become useless in life and could not see again; after all, the snake had not been found and killed.

He saw the whole thing as the talk of a deranged mind. He wondered if anybody was, indeed, behind Adanne's predicament—someone who didn't want to stop with making her blind but also wanted to make her mad. He worried himself over how she would fare if she were mad and blind. And he cried to the Lord God for mercy, while sympathizing with his innocent child, who had never offended anyone. She had led a life of diligence and had never violated anybody's right.

Adanne believed that, with the help of the eyeglasses, she would have relief. And she pressed harder for the eyeglasses, forgetting the condition of the family, who feasted in poverty. This compels her father to believe that her mental state was failing.

He wondered how, even without sight, Adanne could forget the state of her family's finances. He dismissed her requests as one speaking from the gallows.

The most unspeakable part of Adanne's predicament was that, if the snake was caught and killed, perhaps in another village, its end may have come without Adanne eating food prepared with its meat. That would entail that her condition would remain this way, uncured, which made the whole thing crazy.

This new round of Adanne's restive state touched her mother deeply, especially as her daughter's predicament had affected the life the family had all sought after dearly. Though Adanne had already lost the virtuous state of innocence in terms of derogatory displays, this time, she added insidiousness to her outbursts.

Her mother would always be in a bad mood and would sob silently as Adanne raged, cursing everybody and everything she could remember. Her mother never reproved her for her outbursts, as she understood everything and cried along with her.

Her father was not ready to comprehend what she was going through and reason along with her. Instead, he yelled at her, not worrying how she would feel when he called her demeaning names and adding to her present predicament.

Adanne sat in the small hut (*obi*) and cried every day. She retired to bed when everyone had gone to sleep and only after several pleadings from her mother for her to come in. Sometimes this would be in the middle of the night, and she'd come in only to give her mother peace when her mother wouldn't agree to go inside, leaving her outside.

In the morning, she would remain outside and go back to the hut and stay at the time that they would give her food. She would often reject the food, which irked her father and made him more furious with her.

When everybody went out, she would stay there and pray, a habit she had developed from childhood. However, the prayers never lasted. She would soon terminate them when she remembered that her ambition had been buried by the disability that had enveloped her, leaving her with no hope in sight.

Her father would always scold her mother for staying around her, admonishing her to leave the "good-for-nothing girl" to do something useful. But her mother, despite her humility and obedience to her husband, would sometimes lose her temper and snap at him, accusing him of being insensitive. He would leave them and go out. She would stay and try to pacify Adanne, making sure that she was in a good mood before going out. This had badly affected her vocation, which supported her husband's worthless petty trading.

Adanne, even though she was engulfed by regret over her sudden predicament, a regret that displayed itself in her rough disposition, still found time to relax and meditate. She would reflect on what she had done with others before evil had come calling, paying an unsolicited and, it seemed, unending visit.

It has been her habitual way of life to meditate. She was always retrospective when it came to the genesis of her family's problems. She would ponder how this gripping poverty had come to settle upon them. At another time, she would envision how comfortably they would live when she had finished school and secured a good job. And she had always felt happy after contrasting these two conditions of her family's life.

Though she had almost given up this silent exercise of the mind, as her present condition had denied the latter and perpetuated the former, she still took the time to think about how to improve her life. She pondered how she could, perhaps, move out from under her disability and become useful once again. But at no time did she get a positive answer that generated her to seek further information on the prospect.

This time, the issue of the eyeglasses seemed to have robbed her of the formation of such good thoughts. With the unfounded belief that her father had absolutely abandoned her, refusing without good reason to get her glasses, she began to think of a way forward.

In one of her moments of meditation on how to help herself, given that she had been rejected, palm nuts came to mind. She recalled the fallen palm nuts the family used to pick in days gone by. She felt elated, in fact ecstatic, as this wonderful idea appeared in her mind.

She realized that, if she started going to the bush to pick palm kernel nuts that fell from the palm trees and cracked out the nuts, she could give them to her mother to sell for her. She might even succeed in raising the money for her eyeglasses. And that would mean a positive development of hope for the realization of the dreams in her life that the devil had scuttled.

With this sharp emergence of a good and undisputed recipe for improving her life, her joy could see no bounds. However, she kept the plan to herself and pretended like nothing had happened. She nearly disclosed her secret when a sharply dissuading thought flashed through her mind—she might get hurt. The notion made her feel berserk, and she almost reacted outwardly.

She felt downcast, and her mood changed instantly. She almost flared up in anger over the loss of the only available and remaining hope. But then a sustaining and subduing thought also appeared, encouraging her with the assurance that the Lord was with her but warning her to desist from attacking anybody, especially her father, if she hoped to succeed in this risky plan. She felt consoled and compelled to move forward. Adanne made up her mind. She got ready and prepared to move. She, of course, needs no one to consult, no one to encourage her but herself. Her mother might be intimidated. But she would definitely be a barrier, as she would discourage her.

She was afraid that her mother would be concerned about her safety. Moreover, she worried that her subconscious mind would unwillingly accept her mother's fears and that her last hope would be crushed without another thought. She believed that, once she set out on her way, no amount of dissuasion would lure her back. On the other hand, if she told her mother about her plans, she might be guilty of stubbornness—by daring to continue after receiving her mother's warning. Thus, she concealed the idea till the very time she planned to set out the next morning.

As the night broke into morning, Adanne got up early as usual. She did all her early-morning self-cleaning and headed out. Everybody thought that she as going to the front hut, where she stayed. Of course, that was her routine. She would get up in the morning and clean herself before heading out to the front small hut, used sometimes for cooking. Eventually, she started staying there. Therefore, nobody would think anything other than that she was heading to the hut, her lamenting closet.

But this time, they were wrong in their speculation—even though there was a strange addition to her normal routine this morning. No one would imagine what the strange addition might mean, as no one's mind even thought about it.

This time, Adanne carried a big basket in her hands, along with a cutlass she had used when she was still going to the farm. She headed for the small track at the back of her house that led to the farmlands. The farmland was a bush where people farmed and harvested the trees standing on their farms. She never talked to anybody, not even to say good morning. By now, this was regular anyway and didn't raise any eyebrows.

Her siblings became curious about her mission as she headed towards the track without looking back. They asked her about her mission, but she kept mute and moved unperturbed, as if they were the ones expelling her from home.

They insisted, raising their voices to query further. This attracted their mother from within. She felt very afraid when she heard their voices—frightening and persisting as they continued with their questions as to Adanne's mission. She rushed from the house, almost stumbling over the basket containing dirty plates that had been used the previous night. Her second eldest, Nnachi, jumped back in fear, asking what she was doing.

Nwayimma started to cry as she came out of the house. She called to Adanne, asking where she was going and telling her to come back. Having intuitively guessed her daughter's mission, she added a warning. "Adanne," she called, sobbing, "come back. You will be hurt. Nobody is going with you. The farmland is lonely, especially this early in the morning."

"I will not come back, Mama. What does anyone want to do with a dirty useless blind girl like me? Leave me, Mama," Adanne replied.

Her mother walked to meet her and held her, cuddling her as she attempted to persuade her to return. But she courageously told her mother about her plan and how it had arisen from inspiration and assured her of her safety.

As her mother continued to hold her and to try to convince her to come back to the house, her father overheard them from inside the house. When he was ready to go to his small shop, he came out of the house. Looking at mother and daughter contemptuously, he shook his head in condemnation of Adanne's stubbornness and dismissed them with a wave of his hand.

Though taciturn in his reaction, he condemned his wife's efforts. To his way of thinking, she was wasting her time talking to the stubborn girl this early morning. According to him, Adanne had chosen the path of self-destruction. He went back into the house, picked up his key, and left the house.

Though he didn't say anything, Adanne observed him by the silence that hovered as he watched them and the sound of his retreating footsteps. Sensing the reaction of her father, who she believed had really changed for the worse, built up her courage. She was more determined to go than ever. "See what Papa is doing. See how he treats me these days because of my condition."

"But you caused it. You know that your father loves you and cares for you. Yet you accused him of disaffection towards you," her mother replied.

"OK," she snapped. "You support him, Mama."

Her mother admonished her for not appreciating her father's efforts, telling her that it was because she could not see that she could not know how much effort her father had poured into seeing that the snake was discovered and killed.

"What about the eyeglasses I asked him for?" Adanne retorted.

"Do you know the condition of this house? That you cannot see does not mean that you cannot understand or that you have forgotten. Where would we get the money for your eyeglasses? The money we borrowed to pay the search parties has not been repaid, and the creditors are beginning to bother us about it."

"Hence, I move to get the money I need myself. I do not blame you or Papa, Mama. I understand. Just let me go and do this, and I'll get the eyeglasses myself. Don't worry, Mama. I will be fine, really. I am familiar with every place I went before my problems set in," Adanne assured her. With that, she turned to leave.

"You are still going?" her mother said in fear. She blessed her with the hope that God would ensure nothing would harm her. Then she went back to the house to sit and sob, meditating on what might happen as Adanne ventured forth alone.

The disturbing images of what might befall her helpless blind daughter that had preoccupied her all morning still affected her as she left the house, running late. Initially, she thought about going to the bush to check on her daughter. But she dismissed the thoughts with the hope and belief that her God would protect her daughter.

Meanwhile, Adanne entered the bush. She picked a lot of palm kernel nuts and returned home even before anybody else had returned and started cracking them. She was very happy about having made a fortune on the first day. It suggested to her that she would succeed in this venture.

On returning from school, her siblings saw her from afar cracking palm kernel nuts and were surprised. They could not believe what they were seeing. They raced to cover the remaining distance so as to confirm what their eyes saw.

As they got to Adanne, they still couldn't believe what they saw. Ada had almost filled a medium plate with cracked palm kernel nuts. Ada noticed her siblings' presence and felt happy. She greeted them warmly, so different from her mute answer to their greetings in the past whenever they returned from school.

Adanne had cracked enough nuts to generate a reasonable amount of money, and her siblings were happy for her, though they weren't yet aware of her reason for doing it. After the exchange of greetings, Adanne continued cracking the nuts.

The youngest of her siblings, who was about six years old, was about to pick some of the kernels from the bowl to eat them. But the eldest, Nnachi scolded her, warning her to drop the nuts. Nnachi explained that maybe Ada wanted to sell them and make money.

Adanne stopped him, telling him to allow her to eat a few of the kernels. Next, the eight-year-old started asking for his own. Adanne, still happy, asked them to pick about five nuts each to go.

Her siblings—all but one, that is—were happy to pick out some nuts. The ten-year-old, on the other hand, refused to take even one kernel, though he said that he had taken some when Adanne enquired if he had. He was not happy that his siblings were taking Adanne's nuts, so he chased them away.

Adanne continued going to the bushes to pick palm kernel nuts to crack. Her mother would then carry the cracked nuts to the market for sale and keep the money for her. This was a development that began to feel really good.

Adanne never relented, especially as she saw that her efforts would pay off. God willing, she believed that she would raise enough money to get her glasses. Though he applauded her efforts, her father dismissed her plan. To him, custom demanded that, unless the snake was found and killed and Adanne ate food prepared with the meat, she wouldn't be able to see again. Thus, the idea of the glasses was a mirage.

Nevertheless, he didn't intend to dissuade her efforts. After all, she went and came back safely. There was nothing wrong in her picking and selling the kernels, instead of sitting at home and creating a disturbing atmosphere that had made the environment a repulsive one. But as for the eyeglasses and Adanne regaining her sight, to him, it was just a mirage indeed.

His major interest was the help that had come from gathering and cracking the nuts—an effort that now augmented the family's welfare in a small measure. He actually didn't say much about the new development, which had not only given glimpses of Ada's possible return to school but also did not fail to lift the family's spirit.

Having gathered the kernels for a reasonable amount of time, Adanne approached her mother about her desire to get eyeglasses. This was, after all, the reason she had taken the pain. Her mother agreed. Together, they brought the issue to her father, who unwillingly gave his consent. He maintained the belief that this was a sheer waste of funds. But he raised no objection because the money was not coming from him and also to avoid igniting Adanne's intolerable rage.

The day came for Adanne and her mother to go and to get the eyeglasses. They traveled to a town where there was an eye clinic, following the directions someone had given them. They had left very early, and so they arrived at the clinic just as it was opening and took the first seat.

After a series of tests, the officials at the eye clinic—without reassuring them—prescribed some glasses for Adanne, to be collected in about two weeks. Mother and daughter paid for everything in full and left the clinic.

One spectacular thing did occur during the journey to get Adanne the eyeglasses. The clinic staff, especially the chief optician, did not see anything wrong with Ada's eyes, and her blindness left him bewildered. In all the tests that were ran on her, he observed nothing wrong—certainly nothing that would cause her to lose her sight.

Adanne and her mother kept the cause of the blindness to themselves. They wanted to avoid stigmatization and consequent unceremonious dismissal, which would finally mean the end of the search for Adanne's sight. They claimed that she had simply suddenly found herself blind after waking from sleep.

This convinced the officials that her blindness was a result of witchcraft, and that buttressed their conviction that nothing was wrong with her sight. They sympathized with the beautiful girl. Adanne had started regaining her physical appearance since she had found solace in the hope of regaining a bit of her sight with the glasses in mind.

Soon, the day of her appointment to collect the glasses arrived. Adanne and her mother traveled again to the eye clinic in the town where she was being treated to collect the eyeglasses as promised by the clinic. There, the clinic staff got the glasses and tested then on her.

Behold! It was a moment of joy, as the glasses did improve Adanne's power of sight. She regained a bit of her sight, though it remained faint. She could now view people and see a little of the characters in a book.

This changed the atmosphere in Mazi Udenwa's house. Peace and joy returned to the house. Now they could talk together again. While Adanne had not required aid in her every movement before the glasses, she was now fully independent in her movement. She took on some domestic chores, as well as continuing with her job of gathering and cracking nuts—now at a faster rate.

However, a bit up discomforting drama surfaced again when she came up with the idea of returning to school to continue her studies. This did not go over well with her father, who vehemently opposed the proposal.

When Adanne introduced her idea after dinner one night, as planned with her mother, her father cut in and vehemently opposed her return to school. He, thereby, nearly risked a return to the disquiet that had previously left the house. He saw school for Adanne as a sheer waste of time and funds, when he had not even paid for the instruction materials and fees of her other siblings, who were without disabilities.

He simply assumed that there never again be even a slim hope in Adanne's life. Thus, the idea should be discarded without any second thoughts. Mazi Ude reminded Adanne and her mother of his poor state of life. He noted that he couldn't even adequately care for his healthy children, to say nothing of adding expenses for the one whose life has already settled with hopelessness.

But upon realizing that nothing was being demanded of him—in fact, Adanne could now contribute to the family's welfare, along with paying her school fees with her once despised vocation—he shrugged. He agreed to the idea, though he didn't fail to remind them that he didn't have a kobo to offer. Adanne and her mother accepted this, without reminding him that Adanne could take care of her school costs and still assist the family. She had been doing so ever since she started her vocation.

Adanne, whose last joy had been the good news that the glasses improved her sight, was now happy again. She played with her siblings like she had before she had gone blind. She took up the domestic chores she had stopped doing, not because of her lack of sight but due to emotional pressure and discomfort.

She could now socialize again, even with her former schoolmates, who had stopped visiting her when they had grown tired of her lack of appreciation. Actually, she had never wanted to see them. Their visits generated reminders of school activities that were lost to her. At the time, their visits and the accompanying sympathies were not welcome. She had seen them as repugnant and disheartening.

She was now lively. And she assured her father that he would have no involvement in her going back to school. This allayed his fears of incurring more expenses. He hadn't even paid back all the loans he had taken out to pay the search parties that had engaged in searching out the hidden place of the snake in Otoko village. She told him that, in the same way she had earned the money for the eyeglasses, she would earn the money to pay her fees, as her God never slept.

This new voice of Adanne turned the whole family around. They could now laugh again and enjoy the real taste of the food they put in their mouths.

Mazi only reluctantly nodded his head in acceptance. He conditionally aligned with the family, provided he was not required to contribute to the school demands, even the least. He would not supply even a pen. Nwayimma, on the other hand, who had no good means of income, assured Adanne of her support. This baffled her husband. He wondered where she would get the little to offer, not knowing that a woman knows how to keep secrets.

Mazi carried the burden of his wife's assurances in his heart. He wondered if there was anything she and Adanne were hiding from him. That seemed possible, judging from his wife's subsistence farming and poor vegetable sales trade. These two nearly dead vocations were made worse by the catastrophic effect of Adanne's condition. He decided to relax in sufferance and wait and see, though he did pray for his daughter's success. He tried not to think how, if his wife did have anything to offer, it could better have been used on the others. For Adanne, sadly, had been created anew by fate for sorrow.

Adanne reassured her doubting father of her readiness to face the task and that she did not need any outside assistance. In addition, she repented of her loathing towards God in the dilapidated state of mind her illness had engendered. She repented, too, for her blasphemous posture towards the sanctity of God. She decided to go for confession, which she had not done for a very long time. There, she would renew her state of morality before God and prepare herself to start receiving Holy Communion again.

She continued picking palm nuts. That way, she would have sufficient funds to face any emerging problems that would require her father to step in when she went back to school. She actually didn't want anything that would threaten or, worse still, destroy again the good relationships that had returned to the family.

She was very scared of losing the family unity and humor that had been elusive since she'd had her problems and that the acquisition of her eyeglasses had reinstated. Thus, she didn't want her father to so much as come close to any monetary issues regarding her re-enrolment in school. She had seen that, from the onset, he had been quite inimical to the prospect of her returning to school (especially if that required his financial assistance).

As school resumed after the vacation, Adanne got ready for school again. She was like a bride, curiously waiting for her groom to come and take her home, especially if the body was hot and longing for the meeting.

When the school had closed for the holiday, Adanne had counted down the days until it will reopen. So great was her anticipation, that often, without even realizing it, she would soliloquize about her return to school. Of course, this made sense, considering the magnitude of her interest in education and the trauma she suffered when all her hopes seemed evasive. Hence, she had intensified her efforts during the holidays, searching for and cracking nuts at a rapid pace, in order to earn as much money as she could. She had become as eager for the day that school would restart as someone who had never been to school before, especially when her siblings told her of the interesting events that had taken place since she'd left. They had not told her of these happenings in the past due to her wild anger that had made them avoid her.

On the long awaited day, Adanne awoke earlier and began to sing a very sensational Christian song that praised God for His unfailing mercies to the world. This song filled and enraptured her family as it vibrated through their brains. It seemed to them like a trance or a dream before they finally woke up to see that it was a reality and that it came from Adanne. Singing in the morning had once been a habit of hers, before it was swallowed by the sudden change in her life.

Her mother joined her. But her father, who had still not honestly given his approval of her return to school, only grumbled inwardly.

Adanne then got ready along with her siblings and left for school with them.

It was quite a memorable experience to step into the school compound, even though she had lost nearly three years. Her former classmates were almost finishing their JSS 2 class, while she remained in basic six. This, however, it did not in any way deter her.

The school celebrated her return with fun and pleasantries. The teachers who had not been transferred came out to hug and encourage her. The teacher whose work the students had gone to do on the day of the incident had been transferred. So she was not there, though she had visited frequently before leaving.

Some new teachers had transferred to the school after Adanne had left. They had heard all the stories surrounding her life and appreciated her. Though they hadn't come out to see her, they joined the old ones in thanking God for her and in applauding her courage.

Adanne's return was a reception and celebration, replete with an outpouring of joyful noise that rent the air. Everybody stood—an ovation to God's greatness.

Then Adanne got settled back to her studies, working with the partial sight provided by the eyeglasses she had recently acquired. The school authority complemented God's grace by being unusually kind to her. She was exempted from all the menial work in the school curriculum. She was not to do anything that required physical strength, such as bringing a broom, which was done every last Friday of the month; fetching firewood or water for any teacher; or bringing sticks to support the yam stems in the garden. She was also not involved in bringing sticks for making the school's fence or raffia palm for repairing the toilet or some damaged parts of the school building. In fact, she was absolutely exempted from anything that had to do with physical exertion, including the sports she had led when she had been healthy and complete.

Adanne could not hold back tears of joy upon learning of the outstanding generosity the school had shown her. Thus, she settled down without allowing the taunts about her losing nearly three years and trailing far behind her mates to disturb or distract her.

Adanne already had an antidote to such a mental detractor, which tried to feed on her and quench the good news that had remodeled her life, making her once again at least appreciably useful. She kept this reminder in her mind and on hand: *After all, God is not indebted to me. What if I didn't have this second chance? Would it not be a colossal loss?* She was able, quite able in fact, to surmount the monster that had constituted itself into a great and insidious foe.

The visible grace by the school authority increased her joy and her hope for at least a partial realization of her life's aspiration. She dutifully settled down to study. Of course, she self-isolated in the midst of students who were younger than her. She would not allow them to miff her or interfere with her peace.

Though she tried to avoid these young pupils—this time not because of regrets related to her predicament but to avoid anything that would cause them to insult her—they were still all over her. They would ask her assistance with their academic work. Nonetheless, with her younger brother Nnachi being in the same class with her, she felt safe and okay.

She used the opportunity of her exemption from the physical work in school to intensify her work searching and cracking nuts. She considered that, if she had not been excused from the work, she would be working alongside the others during that time period. Thus, she used the time that would have been used to go for a broom to sell her nuts and make money. Her palm nut trade increased in volume. It was soon a thriving and extremely successfully operation.

Customers would even come down to their place to buy and would demand more than her mother could carry to the market.

Adanne's trade triumphed as she added the picking of ripe palm nuts that fell from the palm trees. This had actually been a part of the operation before, though she didn't fully concentrate on it until her palm kernel nut business had enjoyed such success, thus reducing the availability of the kernels. In addition, the supply was reduced by the cutting of the palm heads by the owners, when they were informed of their ripe palm heads by concerned neighbors. She visited the palm trees almost on a daily basis.

Adanne extended her visits, traveling farther than the usual family farmlands with the unfailing aid of her eyeglasses. Soon, all palm oil producers had become her customers. She sold the ripe palm nuts she picked to them. This development increased both her earnings and her joy.

She could now boast of enough savings for her school fees and other academic expenses, as well as for her extracurricular demands, such as clothing and shoes. In addition, she could continue the usual assistance towards supporting the family welfare.

This appreciable savings of Adanne's, which her mother held for her, attracted her father's attention. He would stealthily go to her mother to take a quick loan from it whenever he wanted to go to the market to get wares for his petty provision shop trade. He usually borrowed from a close friend but paid his friend back as agreed. That made it possible for him to succeed each time he approached the man.

Nwayimma would not give Mazi the money without first reminding him of his untoward attitude towards Adanne. She did not do this to indict or scold him but to stage a mild drama that would justify Adanne's usefulness in life as she softly opposed by him. And Mazi Ude would speak in a low tone, apologizing, and get the loan. He would jeer playfully before leaving.

Though Adanne would not have said no had she become aware of the borrowing—she did not, after all, hold a grudge against her father—the loans were made in secret. This kept his respect intact and enabled him to enjoy the worthy benefaction from his disabled daughter, whose life consciously revolved around self-development and independence.

The time came for the Common Entrance Examination for enrolment into the secondary school. Although Adanne had already sat for the exam before her predicament, she would take it again. Adanne only informed her parents that she would be doing so, as she was capable of footing the bill.

Of course, she had remained steady in her excellent performance when it came to schoolwork, despite her disability. She was not quite up to the level she had occupied when she was "complete." But she didn't go back that much. She lost the uncontested first position only to a boy whose parents had relocated to the village from town, though not without healthy competition between the two to outdo each other.

Adanne's announcement that she would be taking the Common Entrance Examination did not go down well with her father. He still believed that she should have ended her education with primary education, since there was no possible hope for her.

As usual, he did not say anything concerning the sponsorship, as Adanne was capable of fending for herself, but only referred to her health condition. His ostensible argument was his belief that Adanne should have allowed the others go, especially her immediate younger brother, Nnachi, who was in the same class with her.

Adanne assured her father of her seriousness about her academic course and her ability to pay the bills. Mazi Ude begrudgingly consented, for fear of bringing to an end the unity and peace that had reigned in the family since Adanne had gone back to school. Still, he would not lose sleep over what he saw as an unattainable desire.

He was guided by the apology he had made to Adanne over his nonchalant attitude towards her in the past. Adanne had not accepted the apology, instead blaming the situation on her restiveness. She had claimed that she was the one to apologize.

Adanne succeeded in pacifying the worries of Mazi Udenwa and warding off the gradual build-up to unhealthy disagreement between father and daughter again. She assured him that she only wanted to test out secondary education and promised that, if the money ran out halfway through the course, she would withdraw. Nevertheless, her intention was to confidently make more money.

In addition, she and her mother refused to disclose her worth to her father. She had actually made enough to cover the expenses. However, just as they always did, she and her mother decided to declare only a quarter of her earnings to him.

Her father was convinced and gave his blessings to the project. This resulted in smiles all around.

Adanne took the examination. As expected, she passed and enrolled in the only secondary school around the neighborhood, which served almost ten villages.

Naturally, one would be worried about how she would make her way to the school from her village. The school was located a distance from the ancient community from which their village had been carved. This led to another round of worry. But the concern was duly solved by God, with her admission being at the same time as that of Nnachi, who would go to the school along with her.

Thus, her eyeglasses and Nnachi formed the two indispensable companions that aided her secondary school program. They always left early on foot, since there was no money for them to live around the community in which the school was located.

She met some of her mates from primary school, who had left her in basic six when she'd had her accident. Some of them were now in class two. Others remained in class one, where they had tarried for years, having thus far failed to get promoted to the next class.

Most unbelievable was that some who had mocked her good conduct and ostensibly rejoiced at her predicament appeared to be facing an end to their school issues even before she enrolled in the school—as they were now preparing to drop out of the program.

Despite their having gloated over her predicament, Adanne did not refrain from giving them the best of her assistance in their academic work. This aid saw them cross into the next year after repeating the class twice. She was still her generous self. Her predicament had not transformed her sound mental ability or her love for her fellow human beings—qualities that made those who were real victims feel relieved after relating to her.

Her generous assistance to these students extended to include those from other communities, who she had not previously known. This so impressed one of the students she had assisted that the student offered to pick her up every morning on her bicycle and take her to school. That way, she could teach her orally as they rode.

This girl was quite serious and came from an average family that was also serious about her education. But she lacked brilliance. Finding and befriending Adanne was a big relief to her. Sadly, though, this friendship did not last, because the girl left town to join her elder brother after the first term.

Adanne felt the termination of this generosity deeply. To her, the ride to school had been the first mercy from humankind in life and had much enhanced her academic pursuit. Even though a girl from her village who had a bicycle and who was among her beneficiaries offered to help two times a week, she rejected the offer for the obvious reasons of avoiding trash. She realized that the offer was made mainly to mock her and not based on genuine feelings for her.

Yet she did not stop assisting the other students. They flooded her locker in large numbers and filled their home, which had been deserted during Adanne's unfortunate incarceration.

Her parents wondered how people could now visit their isolated hut, all because of Adanne's generosity to their academic needs and felt happy with this development. Her father often wondered that the world was larger than man. That Adanne who had no sight was the one leading those who had useful bulging eyes was, indeed, a wonder.

Her performance continued to be excellent, despite her lack of any bridge to aid with her disability. So too did she continue to have the full admiration of many of the teachers. Finally, she completed her program, finishing with excellent results.

As Adanne finished up secondary school, she prepared herself mentally to go on to a higher institution. She decided to sit for the JAMB (the Joint Admissions and Matriculations Board). The

JAMB determined whether prospective undergraduates could enter universities. She reasoned that she had serious good luck to back up this decision. After all, she had seen the grace of God truly manifesting in all spheres of her life.

Her whole being longed for the journey of continuing her education, but her family never thought in that direction. Nnachi had observed her body language, but he was restrained by fear from relating what he had noticed to his parents, especially his father. He knew his father would flare up again in anger and that he would surely resist Adanne's new plan with everything he had this time.

But Adanne, who in turn had observed her brother, never bothered about their father's reaction. Rather, she prepared for a showdown. She built up her spirit for resilience, making herself ready for the imminent clash. Her spirit assured her of victory and advised her on how to approach the issue, without allowing it to degenerate into another round of disagreeable battle.

As she prepared to break the news, she determined a showdown could be avoided if wisdom was applied. Still, she feared the part her mother would play and, thus, spoke to her in confidence. After all, she was the custodian of her finances.

Early one fateful morning, she woke up her parents to announce the resolute desire that had been preventing her from having a good night's sleep. She spoke mildly with a very captivating voice, assuring them of victory at last.

Mazi Ude felt Adanne's proposal to continue her education like a blow to the head. When Adanne had finished her speech, he refused outright to contemplate her furthering her studies after secondary school, especially now that she was a touched human whose life would be better spent with a smile as she picked palm nuts—a path the Lord had shown her. Though Mazi Udenwa openly opposed her plan, he did so without ranting. Rather, he lay out clearly his belief that the proposal was unattainable, trying to make them understand. His ostensible fear was that, if Adanne's money ran out halfway through the program, he would be required to take over the financial burden from there. This was a burden he would not be capable of handling, and he hoped to avert the possibility that it would ever come to that.

His fears were justified by the fact that Ada would not live in the village while she attended school like she had during primary and secondary school. That arrangement had enabled her to keep up her palm nut trade. She would, instead, live in the school and, thus, lose this rare grace. He wondered how she could feasibly continue to pay her expenses.

After all, she had almost been finished by life. Her younger brother never thought of any such plans. He was not brilliant. But even if he was, there would be no reason to stoke the fires of such a rare gem.

Adanne's confidante, her mother, though taciturn, entertained fears that aligned with those of her husband. She actually knew that Ada had some money saved up. But she was afraid of where the money would actually get to considering the size of the project. Plus, she worried over the certainty of the loss of Ada's source of income. She would be living at the school, and she would not be able to find bushes for picking nuts over there.

She cried at the sign of the possible return of disquietude to the house. That intolerable situation was gone, thanks to God, and she did not wish for it to return.

Adanne, however, remained optimistic. She reassured her parents there would be no inkling of problem for them to worry about, reiterating that God had been faithful, even when life had temporarily been like a nightmare. She reminded her father of his opposition to her returning to school and to getting glasses and that he had also opposed her going to secondary school. She pointed out that she had completed both now and, on each occasion, God had shown Himself, and she had triumphed.

She asked her father rhetorically how much he had contributed to these past three projects that he had opposed out of fear of money. This hit her father like a rocket, and he shrugged and immediately expressed that he was in agreement with the plan. He did so, however, with a most bitter feeling that actually frightened Nwayimma, as she saw in it the prospect of the unsolicited return of the long absent squabbles.

As the agreement was struck without reservations, Adanne again rose to the occasion. She assured her parents that before her money ran out, she would discover another source of income. Moreover, she added, she was not the one doing it. Rather, God the Father in heaven had not closed his eyes on her.

"Oh yes! He doesn't close His eye, but where ..." Mazi cut in, before letting his words trail off. He realized that, if he completed the sentence, uninvited trouble might loom in the near future.

His wife sneered at him, and he used his palm to cover his mouth. Then he revised his words, explaining that he meant to ask where the devil lived that he could see Adanne when God went without sleep for her sake.

Adanne, not wanting to read meaning into her father's partially spoken statement, agreed with him and reassured him of God's never-ending love, despite her challenges. Those challenges, she explained, were meant to test her faith and place her where she belonged.

"But you ..." Mazi Udenwa stopped again. He'd almost started to say that she had failed. But he realized what he was about to say, so he decided to stand up and leave. He was afraid that, if he remained there, he might be moved by his restless mind to utter a statement that would dislodge the costly achieved peace. "I am in full support, Adanne. Your God will see you through," he said as he stood to leave the room.

Adanne and her mother were filled with happiness over the discussion. It had gone successfully, and no dissatisfaction had intruded.

"But Papa seems averse to this, Mother. You heard the statements he was trying to make," Adanne said.

"No. You only misinterpreted everything. How I wish you'd had your glasses to see how your father beamed with smiles of satisfaction," her mother replied deceptively.

"Really?" Adanne asked.

"I could not deceive you," answered her mother.

Adanne prepared for the JAMB. She sat for it without Nnachi and passed. She chose the polytechnic closer to them in place of a university for the advantage of proximity. Otherwise, she would have been able to get into any school she chose. She was offered admission to study laboratory technology.

This elicited another round of joy for Adanne, whose beautiful physique and wellness had returned—except for her full sight, which remained elusive. Having only partial sight did not give her the disturbance her blindness once had, now that she had her life back on track. She was astoundingly happy, with no reason to be sad again. Her eyeglasses had proved to be of immeasurable worth. They had been of great service to her and she was deeply grateful for them.

Having been offered admission at a nearby polytechnic, she went to the campus. She chose the laboratory technology course because of its relevance in the medical field. It was Adanne's ambition to study medicine so she could repay God in humanitarian service for giving her back a portion of her vision.

She felt that she needed to be a direct attendant to human health. She wanted to help save those who would have lost their lives due to lack of or inadequate medical attention. She had observed the devastation that could have caused during her treatment after the snake attack if not for God's mercy.

But her ambition to study medicine was thwarted, first by her inability to pay for the expensive course and, second, by her decision to study at the nearby polytechnic, which did not offer a course in medicine. So she settled for the laboratory technology program. She believed that it was related to medicine. Plus, it would afford her the opportunity to continue studying medicine in the future through the experience she would acquire by way of employment in the field.

She was set to leave for the campus. But she didn't know how to get there so she asked for directions. This prompted somebody to tell her that a boy in the next village was currently studying at the school and might be of good help in that respect.

She felt highly favored and set out with Nnachi in the direction of the boy's village. By coincidence, the boy had come back from school to visit that very weekend. Initially, they had gone without the certainty of meeting him but with the belief that somebody in the compound may know how to contact him or how to get to the school. Perhaps they could find someone who had attended his matriculation, which had taken place less than a year ago.

When Ada and her brother arrived in the next village, she enquired after the boy. Shortly, he came out proudly to receive them. She kept quiet as her brother asked for directions to the campus. He supplied the information, but not without mocking them.

"You want to go to the polytechnic? Which of you, if I may ask?" the boy asked.

"My sister here. She just got admitted into the school, but we do not know the directions to the school," Nnachi replied.

"Who told you that they would take her with this disgusting disability? They have rejected even able-bodied applicants, to say nothing of a blind person," the boy said, frowning. He looked at them with an expression of contempt.

"But that is not in your own hands. We only ask that you give us directions," Adanne replied, as Nnachi was afraid or, rather, pressured by his shyness not to say anything further.

"But you do not understand. As a less than able person, she is not qualified. Or do you think that federal polytechnic is for everything that flies into it?" the boy fired back, as if he had never before seen a disabled person in his school. (He had, though those he had seen had disabilities that affected other parts of their bodies, rather than vision impairment.)

Adanne intuitively read the boy's jealousy. She realized that the boy was conceited about being an undergraduate, which was rare in those days. He believed that Adanne attending the same school would spoil his pride in being the only boy from the neighborhood who was studying at the school—a pride he didn't want to share with anybody. Having instinctually noticed this, Adanne grew more energized to press forward and ask him her questions. Her realization about him encouraged her. Ordinarily, one would think that she would be discouraged and would leave with sadness. Rather she was more determined than ever.

Such situations, instead of discouraging Adanne, strengthened her, as her disability was her strength. Initially, she was almost beaten down by the boy's froward attitude towards her. However, having built a great wall of resilience around her ever since she had gotten her eyeglasses and had been able to finish her secondary education unaided, she felt she needed no man to succeed in life, save God as used by her. God was the only one who would be a solace to her and not a sorrow.

The boy unwillingly took out a pen and wrote down the directions, which could also be given orally. Getting to the school involved two or three different vehicles from the motor garage at the community center.

She thanked him for obliging her. But she did not fail to make him understand that life and success did not depend on sight, but on the capability of the mind to reason, react, and reach out. The boy nods contemptuously as he went back into his room, without even acknowledging her appreciation.

Adanne's brother watched the boy in disbelief. He was disconcerted by the boy's untoward attitude towards them, and he deeply regretted the poor financial state of his family. Silently, he prayed that God would help his sister. He hoped that the prayer would not be immediately dismissed, given his loss of faith due to the seeming impossibility of Adanne succeeding with her condition.

He regretted that he did not have the academic resourcefulness of Adanne. That would have possibly enabled him go to the school instead of her. He moaned in regret as he stood speechless, watching the proud boy stepping back into his home. Adanne, realizing her brother's emotional state, took his hand, letting him know it was time for them to go and assuring him of God's interest in the poor.

"But what, Nnachi?" Adanne asked. "Would you fight him because he feels complete and comfortable, forgetting that the same God sees all and directs His actions to encompass all? Our parents have been hard-working, not indulging in evil or corruption, yet they remain very poor. God knows why. Do not be disturbed, my brother. It will definitely be all right one day, just one day. In my blindness, I can see more of the future than you people see with sight. Relax. Do not do anything rash or try to blaspheme God. I tell you this out of experience. Even though I did not do anything rash, I blasphemed against God. And even though I know that I am forgiven, it still hurts me even to this day."

Brother and sister made it to leave the compound. Just then, the boy drew open his curtain, peering at them from the window and mocking them. But they make no reply and left in earnest. They wanted to avoid responding to him, knowing that doing so may well degenerate into quarreling.

Adanne advised Nnachi not to tell their parents, especially their father, what had happened. He obliged her, even though he still wasn't comfortable with Adanne going to the campus alone. He feared the maltreatment that may be awaiting her there.

As Adanne was getting ready to go, he suggested that he could accompany her to the campus at least this first time. But Adanne vehemently opposed the proposal. She pointed out that she was going to live there alone, without Nnachi. It would be better for her to start sorting herself out now without depending on anybody. She assured him that, with the aid of her glasses, she was equal to any situation that might emerge.

Her mother supported Nnachi after he hinted to her about what had transpired at the boy's place, which brought her mother down. Adanne still rejected the offer, even after she realized that Nnachi had told their mother about the incident at the boy's house, though she did not feel bad about it.

The family very much anticipated that Adanne may find similar conditions when she traveled to and arrived at campus and insisted on Nnachi going with her for the first time at least. Nonetheless, she remained quite adamant that she would go alone, and they finally agreed with her.

Chapter Two

Adanne on the Campus

Adanne waited in anxiety for the day to break so she could leave for school. She had prepared everything. In fact, every prerequisite for the admission was in its place, waiting for use at the appropriate time, which was no longer even twenty-four hours away.

She was full of joy—so much that she had been unable to denied sleep that night. All she could think about was that she would finally be enrolling in a higher institution of learning. That joy was enhanced by the inability of her sudden disability to frustrate her singular desire in life. Her education was an aspiration that had no alternative as far as she was concerned. Nor would there be solace to match the magnitude of pain if the achievement was lost to her.

As the day broke and the night gave way to the long awaited morning, Adanne sat up in bed, where she had lain not really sleeping all through the night. She hurried to take her bath. Then she got out her small handbag, ensuring that it contained all the needed documents to facilitate her registration. To avoid any foreseeable problems, she had made sure nothing was left out, though she'd had to start arranging everything the previous night with the help of Nnachi. Of course, she had to be well prepared, considering her condition. As her people would say, "When in haste, do not use the time to guess and try shortcuts."

She was well-prepared and ready to go by the time she bid her family farewell and left with Nnachi for the motor garage. Getting to the garage was a very good trek, and all the while Nnachi insisted on accompanying her to the campus to ease her registration process. But Adanne remained obstinate. She had made her stand. She needed no help at this time. She promised Nnachi a visit as soon as she settled down. She reassured Nnachi that God, in His endless mercy, would see her through.

Finally, they arrived at the garage located at the community's central market, which was regarded as their town. Adanne, following the directions the boy had unwillingly given her, boarded the vehicle going to the first town along her journey to the campus.

In a few minutes, the vehicle filled up, since some passengers had already boarded the vehicle before her arrival. The conductor collected the passengers' fares. Nnachi remained till the last minute of her departure, continuing to insist on going with her. But this time, Adanne had not replied, thus showing her resolute disapproval the entire time the vehicle was filling up.

At last, the vehicle departed, and Nnachi headed home. As the journey progressed, Adanne felt ecstatic. She was going to the campus. She was so cautious that the moment she paid her fare, she removed her eyeglasses and kept them in her handbag, where she had her documents and money. This was done to avoid anything happening to them. She had been told that the road was not smooth and had lots of potholes. The rough road also made the vehicle change gears often, which affected the sitting pattern of the passengers, who moved forward and backward, right and left as the vehicle made its way.

Adanne guessed that anybody, especially the man sitting beside her, could possibly bump into her and knock her eyeglasses from her face while absorbing the shock of the bad road. And this, as it turned out, would not a wrong thought.

As the journey progressed, one kind passenger, who was supposedly going back to the campus, asked her where she was headed. After she learned that Adanne would be going to the campus, so asked if she could be of help. Adanne appreciated her gesture but rejected the offer, her mind set on independence. She had always believed that she could do it alone. It was this same belief that had made her refuse Nnachi's insistence on following her to her destination.

Her instinct told her that God would see her through, and she did not want to complement God's grace with human generosity. She was a very stubborn believer that nothing mattered but God and His unfailing ability and love.

She would trust her eyeglasses over a person and always felt secured in the "hands" of her eyeglasses at least in terms of vision. This made her feel competent to do all the other things that required sight, since her mental sight was unquestionably active and serving her well.

She never wanted anybody to play the role of God for her. After all, she had fervently prayed, and she had seen the manifestations of those prayers. She wanted to always have every genuine reason to glorify Him with unfeigned testimony.

Though the road they were on was very rough, the journey was peaceful and passed on without notable hitches. Just at the expected period of time, the bus arrived at the garage of the first town along her journey. There, the passengers were able to alight, and she could board the vehicle going to the campus.

As the bus arrived, Adanne realized that she needed her eyeglasses now to enable her access the location of the bus going to the campus. Of course, the glasses would help her successfully navigate her way to the bus headed for the campus.

But just as she went to reach her eyeglasses in her bag, she heard the chants of "Poly! Poly!" Since the call was coming from right in front of her, she dismissed the idea of getting her eyeglasses out and shouted, "Poly." The bus attendant answered, "Yes," and helped her enter the bus and settle into a seat in the middle. It was unusual for the bus to load at that point, as students going to the poly always struggled to get to the bus.

This bus driver did not want to wait for his turn and had decided to come up here to load and leave immediately after paying the fine. It was this decision of the driver that favored Adanne. Otherwise, boarding the poly bus, would have required assistance, which she has always rebuffed. She did, however, follow the girl from the previous bus who had offered to help, though she kept her distance to prevent the girl from knowing that she was following her. That would ward off any exaggerated companionship.

The bus filled up and soon left for the journey to the campus. Not every passenger who boarded the bus was going to the poly campus. Some had to travel the route to get to the campus garage and board another bus heading to their destination.

The conductor of the bus asked for the passengers' fares, and Adanne, who God has been leading, put her hand in her bag to get her money. As her people said, "The bag is searched with the mind and not the hand." Therefore, she would not find it difficult to get her money without her eyes.

But as Adanne tried to get her money, she unwittingly pulled out her eyeglasses, which fell to the floor of the bus. She paid her money, collected her balance, and put it back in the bag. Mistakenly, another passenger who sat beside her while pulling his money from his back pocket he adjusted himself, stretching his leg and unknowingly smashing the eyeglasses that were resting on the floor.

Though a clinking sound resulted, nobody guessed that it could be Adanne's eyeglasses. And the journey continued with the conductor collecting his fares.

Worrying that she may not have put the change the conductor gave her away very well, Adanne decided to check it, along with the other contents of her bag. She wanted to be sure everything was intact. She opened the bag, only to discover that her eyeglasses were not in her bag. Curiously, she searched for the glasses, arousing the interest of those sitting around her, as her restlessness became alarming.

The passenger sitting on her left became quite uncomfortable with her worry and asked her what she was looking for.

"My eyeglasses!" she replied frantically. "I had them in my bag, but I cannot find them anywhere. Oh! *Chim o!*"

As she said this, it struck a nearby passenger's mind that she had heard a clinking sound not long ago. She looked on the floor of the bus to see the pieces of the smashed eyeglasses. She shouted thunderously, attracting the attention of the passengers sitting in front and behind them.

The passengers, irked by this outcry, demanded to know why she had let out such an alarming shout. The woman showed them the eyeglasses Adanne was looking for, and the bus became heated with serious emotional reactions. Adanne shouted violently and started crying profusely. Nobody knew what to do or what to tell her.

The man who had smashed the glasses realized immediately that it had happened when he had been trying to pull his money from his back pocket. He offered to replace them. The other passengers applauded his suggestion, seeing that the smashing of the glasses had been a mistake. But Adanne refused the offer; allowing him to replace the glasses would have looked like retaliation on her part.

Adanne vehemently refused to accept anything from the man, despite the many appeals of her fellow passengers, who saw her decision as irrational. After all, it was her sight that was in jeopardy. But Adanne still refused, sobbing emotionally, a display that was very sensational.

The man tried to pacify her, promising to give her whatever she wanted to be comfortable until another pair of eyeglasses could be provided. But she remained obstinate, believing that collecting anything from the man would amount to retaliation.

The man continued pleading with her, considering her condition. But Ada insisted on not collecting anything, maintaining her position until the bus got to the garage and the passengers alighted and dispersed. The man stayed near Adanne, asking her what she wanted. She honestly told him not to worry but to go his way. The man left having exonerated himself of any blame whatsoever, given that he had offered to replace the glasses, but she had refused to accept.

Still, he still felt obligated to help her. So he returned to her side to appeals to her once more. However, she made him understand that she had forgiven him and that she bore no grudge against him—saying that it was the way God wanted it. The man finally left for his destination.

Adanne sat on the corner of the road sobbing emotionally. She pondered how she would get to the registration arena and how to conduct herself there, now that she no longer had her glasses.

Adanne desperately desired the help that had been offered earlier now that she had lost her glasses. It was her glasses that had given her confidence and independence. She didn't know what to do next, as she couldn't see anyone to beckon for help. She could only overhear voices and observe movements.

As she sat there, a kind older student who was heading towards a lecture observed her and her desperation and reached out to her. Adanne felt highly relieved and happy and thanked the student for her gesture.

The student asked Adanne about her mission at the school. Adanne explained that she had come to register at the poly and then told her all about her ordeal and how she had lost her glasses, which helped her see. Moved by passion, the student agreed to help her get to the area where the registration was going on. But she couldn't stay with her because she had lectures to attend. She promised to come back and check on her, which she did not do. Besides, Adanne did not want that, owing to her desire for independence.

Soon Adanne had arrived at the registration ground. There she met a mammoth crowd, which frightened her. The registration had been ongoing for two days now, but the officers were slow and insensitive to the plight of the prospective students, who had nowhere to squat after the long day. They played around in the office and treated the students with unjustified hostility, looking for any who would utter a word about it and expelling him or her.

If the registration officiants had shown passion for their duty and compassion to the intending students who were visiting the school for the first or second time, the crowd would have become smaller by today. This was exactly what Adanne had counted on. It was why she'd delayed her trip for two days, arriving on the third and final day to begin the exercise, which would span a week.

But Adanne's calculation failed her because of the lackadaisical attitude of the registration officers. Though she was not the only disabled student coming to register, hers was a different kind of disability, as it involved sight. That was foreign to the school.

Her arrival was greeted with raised eyebrows by fellow students. Their reactions did not much affect her as the girl who had offered her assistance led her to the queue. She joined in the long line, and the girl left.

Adanne stood firm in her position, cautiously allowing the sensations and noise to guide her, knowing that she had no help. She regretted not allowing Nnachi to come with her but dismisses the thought. After all, she had not known that she was going to lose her eyeglasses, and this absolved her.

Though blind, Adanne was very remarkable. Her beauty stood out. Some people admired her. Others despised her for making an impossible attempt even, as they wondered how she passed the JAMB. Some guessed that someone else might have sat for it on her behalf.

If not for the desperation with which the students followed the process and their curiosity about registering, some who admired her would have probably offered to assist her. But everybody was selfishly concerned about his or her own needs, having waited for a day or two to be registered. Others who had arrived this morning just like her and had heard about the hostile attitude of the officers, as well as their laziness, were preoccupied with how they would manage if they ended up having to pass the night there.

Adanne was, thus, left to her own fate. Some of the prospective students found time to mock her, rather than concentrating on their own worries. They wondered what she was doing there, as the school had no provisions for blind students.

Their murmuring, though in low tones, got to her. But she ignored them, seeing them merely as one of those threats or oppositions trying to rob her of her ambition. She was, instead, encouraged by their ridicules, which she had begun to expect from the time she had gone to the boy in the neighborhood to ask for directions to the school. She had already foreseen the challenge and had gotten ready for it. Hence, she was never daunted by the ridicule, no matter the height of the challenge.

Assuring herself of success since she had gotten this far, she dismissed those who mocked her as ignorant and fidgeting souls who had no experience in life. She regretted that, if she were what God had made her to be in her physical appearance, she would not even be in this polytechnic with them. Rather, she would have been graduating by now. But quickly she shunned her feelings and became invigorated to forge ahead.

She assured herself with one good statement, saying, "I will not give up, no matter the threats of the devil. I will defy fear, deny failure, dig further, and discover the fortune fixed for me." She snorted down sorrow, boosted her courage and occupied her position firmly, while the sluggish exercise progressed without visible progress.

As this went on, everybody concentrated on his or herself and forgot Adanne, who couldn't see what was going on but preoccupied her heart with prayers. She reached out in front of her to observe when the boy in her front had moved up, and she followed.

One irony was that the boy in front of her was not comfortable with her behind him. He guessed that she would be pestering him with her problem and thought of leaving his position to go back. But remembering that he had spent two days on campus without registering and having not even a kobo on him to eat that night should he miss the opportunity to register again today, he endured. He remained in his position. Though he did not complain, he built up skirmishes in his mind over her presence, which he considered as highly questionable.

The prospective students managed with the rough queue under the scorching sun, and Adanne remained completely helpless. Nobody talked to her. And when she so much as enquired of anybody, especially the boy, what was going on, they would not reply. Her heart was beating fast, and she was crying in her heart. She almost reminded herself who she had been before the predicament, but her spirit admonished her, warning her that, if she engaged in such thoughts, she would start crying. That would be worse for her, as nobody was prepared to soothe her. With this spirit, she summoned courage again and fought on.

It was only the boy who occasionally responded to her, owing to the fact that he, too, was forlorn. He shared her state of poverty and would be in the same position as her, if not for the fact that he had sight. This feeling gave him a chill, and he felt for her. Thus, he sometimes responded to her enquires, while rebuffing her at other times.

Having lost her glasses in the bus, Adanne was not fully involved in the whole exercise; in fact, she was not a part of the whole thing. She didn't know the distance remaining in the line—had no idea how much ground was left for her to cover before she would get registered. All she knew was that she was in a queue and at the mercy of the boy in front of her, who reluctantly and rarely kept her updated. She only made sure that she was not pushed out of her position as she stood firmly.

Though bound together with others by the queue, she was isolated, considering the hostile relationship with the other long-faced prospective students, which they had meted out on her. Still, she remained resolute to succeed, even against all odds.

The tension grew more heightened as the evening and the time of closing for the officers gradually drew near. Even though they had been the major cause of the unsuccessfulness of the exercise, with their sluggish and hostile handling of the whole thing, they showed no empathy, even to the most vulnerable in the queue. They didn't care in the least what would become of them.

Consequently, as the closing hours speedily drew near, the atmosphere became charged with anxiety in every student. All of them wanted to get the registration process done today. All hoped to avoid another helpless night passed without help from elsewhere—especially as they were all just strangers, meeting for the first time.

Thus, the rowdiness increased by the second. The hostile officers announced with apathy that they would only register twenty more students, as that was all they had time for before they would close for the day.

This announcement had the impact of throwing a bomb of confusion into the queue. It sparked off a very serious disquietude and loss of decorum. All of the remaining students jostled to be among the lucky twenty students.

The queue was disorganized as the stronger ones struggled to file to the front to be registered. It was like an avalanche of violence as they pushed themselves out of their occupied positions attempting to claim the desired place to be able to get registered.

It was a very difficult situation for the students, who struggled with their last strength. Those who had not eaten since morning were pushed out by energetic students. The former included the boy in front of Adanne, who was only saved from being pushed out by the tight grip of Adanne's hands.

He was only floating on the air and would have fallen like a felled tree if Adanne had left him because he was thin and had not eaten since morning. The strong force of the students attempting to rush past him was thwarted only by Adanne's firm hold.

The apathetic officers remained passive as they watched on with delight, enjoying the volcano of restiveness in the crowd. In fact, they felt it was a good opportunity for entertainment, like watching a movie. They sat back, without even attempting to start the registration of the promised twenty students.

The helpless Adanne, whose only hope had rested from the onset on the providence of decorum, thrust her two hands out and held the boy in front of her with unbreakable determination. As the wrestling for luck raged on, she shouted, "Don't leave me! This is my position. Don't leave me!" If the troubled queue swerved to the right, she would hold the boy to follow it. If it went left, she would steer him in that direction. The boy, meanwhile, didn't even notice her. He didn't immediately realize that her grip was saving him from losing his position—that he would not have succeeded if the turbulent situation had not arisen.

Of course, many students held onto each other in this way. Some males were conscious of the females they were holding or being held by, rather enjoying the trouble and the high emotional state it carried.

As the boy noticed that Adanne, the stigmatized girl, was holding him quite firmly, he became uncomfortable and embarrassed. He tried energetically to push her away, but to no avail.

"Don't leave me! Please don't leave me. My God will bless you," Adanne keeps shouting.

But the boy was not ready to hear her. He tried to push her away, so as to be free from her troubles as he guessed them to be. It even got to a point that he lost interest in the whole thing and even in struggling for the registration. He decided to leave the arena—to call it quits and go home. He had spent two days of no success, and now he was losing the third day again. He didn't have so much as a kobo with him to purchase food to eat or water to drink. He was completely empty apart from the transport fare with which to board back home after the registeration.

He felt that it was not his luck to get this registration done; otherwise he would have succeeded the first day. When the office had closed that day, he had been only twelve people away from registering. And yesterday, there had been only five people to register before it was his turn when the office had closed. Today, again, he had waited, and though the queue was quite long, he had hoped to register. Now pushed backward by the violent queue after the announcement, he was done. He did not have the physical strength or economic resources to continue. He was a wretched boy from a stinking wretched home. He became confused and convinced that no destiny awaited him here at the school.

But ironically, Adanne refused to let him go. She believed that, if she lost him, she was doomed. Though she was unable to determine their exact position, she sensed their closeness to the window of the office.

"Leave me. Let me go. I don't want to register anymore," the boy pleaded.

"No. I will not leave you. Please, do not leave me. You are my only hope here. Please!" Adanne kept shouting, even as the boy tried to fling her away.

Try as he might, he could not shake her, as her grip was strong and unbreakable.

As he tried to free himself, her pleas and cries that he was her only hope would occasionally touch him and break him down. He would gently try to let her know that he wanted to go. Adanne refused to understand what he was telling her, believing it was only a ploy to push her away.

As this madness raged on, the callous officers took advantage of the moment, feeling aroused by the chaos. The boy continued to struggle frantically to push Adanne away. She continued with all her strength to hold him as her only remaining hope, all the while shouting, "Don't push me!" And everybody else, concerned only with the struggle to be among the twenty and unable to afford to be distracted, paid her no heed.

The officers, who had ostensibly made the announcement to stir the crowd in order to find a reason to suspend the day's exercise, simply locked up the registration window and taciturnly announced the end of the day's exercise.

Adanne only heard the screeches of the shutting windows and mistakenly thought that it was the opening of the window to register the promised twenty. Thus she increased her efforts to hold onto the boy, still shouting, "Don't leave me!"

As the windows shut, announcing the end of the day's exercise, the prospective students, filled with the excruciating pain of another day of disappointment, gave up and started to disperse. Adanne did not loose her grip on the boy. "Don't leave me!" she cried again. "My God will reward you. Please don't leave me."

With this end of the day's business, the students who had been fully occupied with the heightened tension and the desire to succeed and thus had not noticed Adanne and the boy, now fully noticed them. Some dejectedly left, paying the two no mind, fuming with rage in their hearts and cursing the officers. Others just moved under the big flower trees to watch the free "movie" starring Adanne and the boy.

Adanne still felt certain that she was being outsmarted by the boy, so she held onto him and continued shouting.

The other students watched on. It was like a deliberate plot to lift their despondent feelings and overpower the rain of curses against the unfeeling officers. As Adanne held the boy, he tried to make her understand that the officers had closed the office for the day and that she should let him go.

Only Adanne and the boy she held hostage remained in the queue. Some of those watching from under the trees advised him to push her out. Others mocked them, calling them Romeo and Juliet and saying they matched each other. "That one is hungry-looking, while the other is blind." They laughed hysterically.

Some who had been relieved of their pains of disappointment by the scene playing out in front of them called the two of them names, telling the boy to bite her so that she would leave him. Adanne would have known that the officers had closed but for the noise these students made in their attempts to persuade the boy to push her. She thought the exercise was still going on and shouted more and more.

"But they have closed now. Just let me go. I beg you. They are no longer registering," the boy told her.

"Please don't leave me. My God will bless you," Adanne pleaded.

"Ha! Which God is that?" the boys mocked.

Sometimes, the boy would want to push her as the other students persuaded him to do. But his instinct, which came from a humble background, would restrain him. He would gently try to make her understand. But Adanne simply saw this as a response to the persuasion for him to push her away.

Some of the rascals even threatened to come and forcefully pull her from the boy, since he was showing undue leniency. But the boy objected to their interference and pleaded with her mildly.

As this drama progressed, the officers watched with gluttonous enthusiasm, especially enjoying the moment when one boy made to force the blind girl loose from the boy. One of the officers snorted, paused, and suggested to others that they should register these two students. At least that would end this embarrassing drama. The blind girl was clearly not willing to leave the haggard-looking boy who was sure to eventually faint in the middle of the arena.

Before he had even finished speaking, the other three officers concurred in sincere agreement, claiming that their conscience has been pricking at them over this. One of them said that he had almost made the exact same suggestion.

The officers felt sorry for the first time. Without wasting time, they opened the window again.

As Adanne heard the screech of the opening window, she lost hope. She thought that the registration officers had shut the window and were done for the day. She snorted down her sorrow and released her grip on the boy. Just then, the other students who were still hanging around rushed to rejoin the queue, believing that the officers only wanted the crowd to thin out before registering the twenty.

When Adanne let go of the boy and he wanted to take to his heels, for fear she would grab hold of him again, one of the officers called out to him, "Hey, you!"

The students rushed forward.

"You with the blind girl," the officer called.

The boy retraced his steps and turned to face the officer.

"Come with your sister," the officer said.

"Eh?" the boy answered, standing like an imbecile with his mouth open and his eyes bulging in disbelief.

"Lead your sister here. I want to register you two," the officer said.

The others struggled towards him, but the officer stopped them, saying, "Wait, all of you. Wait first until I finish registering them. Then I can attend to you."

The gathered students honorably obeyed and stayed quiet as the events rolled out. The boy led Adanne to the window, and the officers registered them both, even helping to gather their credentials so they could register in their various departments. He told them to come and see one of them for their receipts whenever they returned to school.

This was a quite unusual way of registering students, without the officers collecting something from the students in return. Not only did they take care of Adanne and the boy's school registration, they also took on the responsibility of helping them register in their departments, which would have been another round of pain. The officers apologized to the two new students. One dipped his hand into his pocket and drew out a note of legal tender. He gave it to Adanne, urging her to keep up her faith. "Strength can fail," he told her. "But faith does not. For even if strength fails, when faith fares, the result is fortune."

This statement struck Adanne's subconscious mind. She thanked the man and wished him well. The officers shut down the windows again, to the total amazement of all who had seen how things had worked out for these two who had been despised and forlorn.

This time, no mockery and no ridicule ensued. Rather, the students who had witnessed what had happened stared on in obsessed bewilderment, quietly watching the two leave the officer's window. They wished they had been the two despised ones, who now were fully registered bona fide students of the polytechnic. Even the disabled girl had their admiration because she had a unique gift that the abled may not have. Can you imagine the contented ones wishing they were the downtrodden, the disabled, and the forlorn?

As the group watched in awe of the incredible events—in awe of seeing the despised and stigmatized outshining the rest—they embraced and accepted what had taken place. Ucheakachukwu led Adanne away from the arena. The two were admired by those who had once despised them. They walk with confidence in God's presence in their lives, which no one could doubt, given the unusual event that had played out just now.

As the two walked on the path to the gate, Uche sensed a new and unique spirit within him. He could not understand this new feeling that reeled in his heart as he looked at Adanne. He repented of his threat to disown her. She then held him around his waist while he was sincerely feeling absolved for not having yielded to the earlier attempts to push her away.

He could barely contain the joy that filled his heart. With it, he could now tolerate another night in the open. Such a prospect would have been terrible if he had not registered but still had to endure another night without food. Leaving for home that evening would have simply announced the end of the game with education in his life and that of his family.

He tried to unravel what would have transpired. But the more deeply he thought about it, the more lost in confusion he became about what the whole thing would have turned out to be for him. He stared at Adanne, who was also meditating on what had happened. As she had not seen what had transpired, she thought about the feelings and sensations she had experienced.

As the duo meditated, Adanne felt that Ucheaka's silence was a sign of the unraveling of the sadness and embarrassment she had caused him. She believed he had only wanted to lead her out to the road to help her board a bus or to go and leave her to her fate.

"Brother, I know that you are still angry with me for causing you such embarrassment. Please forgive me. I am very sorry. I was desperate and had no other hope. They say if the blind fail to pick the fruit the leg kicks, they cannot get another," Adanne said.

"No, you got it wrong, my sister," Uche replied. "I should be apologizing to you for rejecting you at your most desperate time of need and not even considering your condition."

"But you are not the cause of my predicament," Adanne cut in.

"Nobody talks about the cause now. We talk about the gain," Uche said.

"Are you suggesting that my condition led to the success we had today? What about those registered after us? What—"

"Nobody was registered again after us," Uche told her. "They shut the windows after they registered us, and that finally marked the end of the day's business."

"You mean this?" Adanne asks.

"My sister, leave that talk for another time. My concern now is how we will go from here."

His use of the word *we* and the phrase *another time* cut Adanne's senses, and she felt confusion. She thought to herself what this might certainly mean. Had the boy chosen to be of help? She could not believe her sense of reasoning. She also meditated on the boy's concern for her welfare, as he was worried about how she would go back.

"The Lord will lead me," Ada assures him.

"Yes of course. He has shown that He is able and cares. Yet we must avoid risks to remain safe. We should not tempt God because of the great favor He has just shown us today. It would not be a grace to gull Him."

"What are you implying?" Adanne asked.

Uche paused and reluctantly offered, "I wonder … I don't know if you can follow me to where I squat. It is late already. You can't go, especially … It's just risky."

Ucheaka led Adanne like a partner. Without using her walking stick again, she followed alongside him. They walked together, she like one with sparkling vision. Unless one looked deeper, he would likely not know that she was blind.

Their bodies touched each other, which sent a radiating message of oneness to their minds. They had never before felt this way in all their lives. It was emotionally engrossing. Each felt the other's body was that of an angel. In fact, they were completely swarmed by the feeling of the abode of God, called Paradise. Their brains were filled with this obsession, without an iota of immoral intrusion. Both were devoted and had never imagined such a thing happening in their lives.

Ucheaka could not believe this feeling for another human had eluded his life thus far. Adanne, who took her mother as her beloved, had not felt elsewhere a flash of the sensation she had in his company. They both began to wonder who the other was, without disclosing what they were thinking and feeling to each other.

By intuition, each could feel the other's unfeigned acceptance. But they couldn't confirm this yet. They walked along to the main gate of the campus and discussed what to do next.

Ucheaka was a very poor boy—not poor in spirit or health but in finances. His family was so wretched that the entire village stigmatized them, for fear of being infected with their disease of poverty. If it were said that the air—the natural air they breathe—was borrowed, it would not be an overstatement. The family's entire life depended on dependency and revolved around dependency of no seeming end.

They still lived in a shanty in the community—a shanty so lacking that no one would ever put his tame animals in such a tent. They were affected by erosion when it rained, frozen during the rainy season, and burnt and hot during the dry season. Every life situation that blessed some people would hurt them. They depended on working on others' farmlands and thought only of the one thing—feeding themselves. Nobody discussed anything in the house other than how to feed themselves.

When the robust brilliance of Ucheaka in both academics and natural endowment was despised by the villagers, who were not at all sympathetic to the family's plight, Uche's parents were spurred to take action. They made the lofty and almost unattainable decision to train him in school, no matter what it costs. They would see to his education, even if it meant the sale of the only portion of land they had left on which to put their tent, having mortgaged and sold the rest to save lives attacked by monstrous health challenges in the past.

The education he had thus far attained was sponsored by borrowed funds. For now, the family held onto the farmland they had. Life was a curse to their living.

Ucheaka had an irresistible interest in education. On top of that, he was brilliant. The combination should have made him sought after by the students in the school and should have ensured he would receive assistance given to poor students. He obviously should have stood out. But the stigma the village visited his family caused them not to recognize his brilliance—the brilliance that should have been a benefaction to them. All they knew was that this boy's family carried a perennial disease called poverty that should be avoided at all costs.

It was quite incredible to see that, despite the benefits he might have brought to the village, the villagers still isolated him because of his family's poverty. It was as if they believed it was a state of life that was glued to the family forever—an irremovable curse from the ages past from generation to generation.

"The snail that blinds itself denies itself food." The people of Uche's village were the ones losing. Their children remained of poor academic standing. They continued to underperform and remained stagnant in their academic pursuits—a problem Ucheaka would have solved for them long ago had they allowed him to do so.

As for Uche's family, they accepted their fate. They depended on the only available benefactor, God, whose existence they occasionally doubted. This doubt was not a result of the wretched and disgusting condition of their lives. Rather, it stemmed from the difficulty of tolerating the unprovoked mockeries and jeering meted out on them.

"The hated swallows his ball of food without touching it in the soup, yet they claim that he has finished the soup." Seeing the unrestrained readiness of the village to lynch them, without anyone coming to their rescue or God protecting them, Uche's family moved farther from the village. Their only connection with the villagers was the unavoidable search for hire to work on their farms. This they could not refrain from, lest they all perish of hunger. Despite the loathsomeness of the jeering, the family still stealthily moved close, at least for the sake of daily bread—not received as generosity but as wages for work done.

Mazi Obilo, the father, had been born to a poor father, who had also been born to a poor father who had nothing left for his descendants. The villagers mocked them because of this situation, saying that poverty ran in their lineage. Mazi Obilo had inherited virtually nothing from his father. He had only the dilapidated hut he repaired almost on a weekly basis and no farmland to farm on. Even if there was any, it was already on mortgage for loan.

The man and his wife, Chigere, though stingingly poor, swore to see their son Ucheaka through school. Their primary motivation was not to gain. They had already concluded that it was their unacceptable fate to remain poor, considering God's seeming lack of responsiveness to their pleas. No. They were motivated by determination not to allow this rare brilliance that the boy possesses to become lost and unutilized.

Ucheakachukwu, as they had named him in dismissal of the village's stigmatization, had four younger siblings who rarely went to school due to lack of sponsorship. His siblings, rather, followed their parents to till others' farmland so they could earn enough for daily food and to pay for Ucheaka's education.

They attended school each time school resumed and stopped when driven away for non-payment of school fees. In the past, they had paid the fees in installments, with the encouragement and permission of a former headmaster before he was transferred. This grace had seen them reach a reasonable height before his redeployment. His successor, despite the headmaster's appeal to him on Mazi Obilo's behalf, did not allow the arrangement to continue.

Ucheaka was very quiet and humble; these characteristics were, of course, a compulsion of poverty and the hunger that was his constant companion. He was very respectful and brilliant like Adanne. And he held no grudges against anybody, a trait that lived inherently in the family. Uche's family believed that holding grudges would deprive them of the benefaction they got from soliciting work from the others.

Though Uche's situation was very similar to Adanne's, his family was worse off than hers. This was true at least on the grounds that her parents could provide food and pay their children's school fees. In addition, they had bona fide ownership of some farmlands. Though their land was on mortgage, they did have the hope of redeeming the land. In the case of Uche's parents, their mortgaged lands had almost been acquired by the lenders, in accordance with the agreement that had been made—an agreement his parents had signed having no other option.

Ucheaka's situation also fell below Adanne's as his family lived almost like despised slaves in the village. They received no support from any quarter but sustained constant maltreatment.

Though they had totally resigned themselves to their fate, they couldn't stop struggling with their livelihood based on hired labor. Even this hurt their hearts, as their employers often failed to pay the full wage as agreed. Everyone knew that the family was susceptible to this form of maltreatment, as their situation would not allow them to react. They had no recourse other than to leave it to God.

This day was Uche's third day in the campus. And it was his third day without a glimpse of hope—until the intervention of God that came through the grip of Adanne. For her part, she couldn't interpret the situation. She was not fully conscious of the happenings due to her lack of sight. She could only imagine the environment based on the observations of her other senses, and her imagination couldn't be fully correct.

Uche did not have anything to eat, as he had already run out of money. In addition, he wasn't comfortable going back to the apartment he had been squatting in. He feared that he might have been spotted during the past two days and could be attacked. Though he was not really afraid of dying, he feared how his parents and siblings would receive and respond to the news of his death. The family, even though ravaged by poverty, lived in peace and a oneness breathed into them by God. This helped them deal with their isolation from the rest of the village.

Though Uche was handsome, he looked quite pale and unimpressive. Life's unfriendly circumstances had resolutely swallowed his presentable physique. The agonizing heart of hopelessness engendered by the power wielded by constant hunger and unfulfilled wants had ravaged him.

He recalled the events once more. He had decided to push the blind girl away from him with the last of his strength. But his attempt to loosen the lioness's grip had been futile. So he had resigned to her grip and the jeers of the day until the drama was over and he could return to the dungeon in which he had been squatting.

Now, Ucheaka was filled with joy, an emotion that had long ago abandoned him. He was, in fact, giddy with happiness—not because he had finally succeeded in registering but because the hope that he had lost had returned. His ambition to continue his education had suddenly sprung up again.

He, in fact, loved Adanne with infatuation. He cherished and accepted her as a messiah sent from heaven to resuscitate his lost hope in his only interest in this wicked life—education.

Adanne, for her part, could not hold back her affection for Uche. Though she could not see him, her instinct made her feel relaxed and secure in his presence. This was a feeling that was alien to her—for she had never imagined this love thing, to say nothing of practicing it. Uche's voice, as communicated to her by her heart, was that of a trusted friend, and his body was the body of partner. She prayed fervently that he did not think of jilting her, which was the same prayer that Uche prayed about her.

In fact, the two of them fell in love immediately, as though God had facilitated their love with all that had happened. It was love at first "sight."

But if one judged only from the inexpressible inner feeling of the two lovebirds had for each other, it was far from that. Adanne had no understanding of love that would enable her to recognize it for what it was. Uche was only a timid boy from the bush, whose life revolved around pain. To think of love and its attendant attributes, therefore, was a strange and unique experience. It was something he would have perhaps learned something of on the campus after socializing, not something achievable on his own. Adanne's love was her ambition to go to school and nothing else. Therefore, she would not understand the meaning of what was happening between them even if she had been taught it. The undertone of love or anything about it was, in fact, alien to both of them.

Adanne would probably have had an idea about love if she had entered secondary school as originally planned when she had her sight. But the loss of her sight and the groaning within deprived her of every good feeling about life—so much so that even her brilliance was affected.

The two moved together, holding each other. This caused some amazement. Even though it was not strange to see opposite sex couples on campus holding hands, Adanne's blindness, though not quickly observed, created a slight roar. It was not anybody's business as far as Ucheaka was concerned.

Despite their timid lifestyles, the holding of hands, which was no longer new to them, given what had happened on the queue, caused them no shyness. The sensation that was coming from it blinded them from seeing or hearing the people's reaction. They moved to one corner in the front of the campus beside the main gate to sit down and decide what to do next.

Chapter Three

The Jinx Broken

As they moved out of the campus, with the night falling swiftly and incognizant of their condition, Uche narrated his two-day ordeal on the campus. He told Adanne how he had been struggling to register but to no avail. Adanne narrated her own ordeal. She recounted how she had rebuffed all offers of help, with absolute confidence in her eyeglasses but had most incredibly lost the glasses on the bus.

As they talked more and more, a passionate feeling of affection for each other grew. Uche told Adanne that he had been squatting in a shop balcony without the owner's knowledge.

Adanne quarried whether there were no people occupying the shops, and Uche said, yes, that it seemed that people didn't like the shop or the owner refused to give them out. Ada wondered how a line of shops in this commercially busy campus community would be unoccupied. She was afraid that something might be wrong with them and almost dissuaded Uche from going back there. But Uche dismissed her fears, which were remedied by her unshaking belief in God.

"You are right, Ada. I had not thought of that, though my disposition and helplessness would not let me think of that. My people say, 'One with a purging problem does not recognize the shrine in trying to poo poo.'"

"Of course you didn't. Your mind was only on how to register and go back and face the next stage of moving in," Adanne replied.

"Of course my senses didn't start working for me again until God brought you to me," Uche said.

"What did I do for you?"

"Of course you wouldn't know. With you here, I can even sleep here without being afraid of anything."

"Don't try to make me a demigod. I am not one. How can the blind be of help to the one with sight?"

"You are not blind as far as I am concerned. Moreover, you are no longer blind as long as I am with you. I shall be your sight; your days of painful groping are over."

This statement struck Ada's brain. She wondered what this might mean. Perhaps the boy might be interested in her. That might be the biggest gain she had ever had in life, as she had never before felt relaxed in anybody's arms.

Uche, sensing her meditation, blamed her for thinking otherwise and said that they would not be separated on this campus but would remain together until they were through, especially as they shared the same rejected and dejected background. "Who else would accept us than each other? Why would we separate?"

Ada felt quite uncomfortable about what he had said. Perhaps this boy was taking advantage of her because he had no one else to accept him. But she dismissed the thought immediately, as she assumed she was the one taking advantage of him. After all, despite his poor financial background, he did have his sight. If he chose to go back this night, he could, but she could not. He was able to squat somewhere, but she could not locate a place.

She concluded that she was the one who was in need of this boy. She decided to be more prayerful for him not to leave her. In addition, she would conduct herself in a manner that would encourage him to remain with her, though not on immoral ground. Ucheaka, for his part, had never thought of sensuality in his life. He didn't even know what that would entail or how it would look, sound, or taste.

They talked more passionately as the day gave way to night. Ucheaka suggested that Adanne should follow him to the balcony. They would squat there that night and leave tomorrow.

Adanne felt enthusiastically happy, and she thanked him for such kindness.

"Why are you thanking me? I should be the one thanking you. You brought luck to me. You recalled my hope that had absconded from me. You made me feel like a human again. Think of what would be crossing my mind now if I hadn't registered today—the pain, the agony, the penury. In fact, by this time, every bad and evil thing would have been traversing my mind unperturbed. But here I am jesting and laughing—a laugh I don't think I have had in life except on the day I saw my admission letter."

"Okay! I withdraw. But each of us played a part in the progress we shared. What if you had pushed me away?"

Ucheaka felt pinched by this statement. He remembered how many times he'd decided to push her away yet hadn't for lack of strength to execute it. He felt so guilty that he never wanted to talk about that point again. Instead, he suggested that they go to a bucket to drink water, as he had no money. Then they could stealthily sneak to the balcony and sleep till tomorrow, when they could go home.

But Adanne reminded him of the money the man had given her. She told him that they could use it to eat, as neither of them had eaten since morning. Ucheaka remembered and felt extremely happy, and they leave for a restaurant, where they would eat before heading to the balcony.

The owner of the compound housing the long balcony of the ten unoccupied shops in the very strategic business corner, Chief Otieke, was an extremely wicked man. He had no qualms whatsoever about shooting people. He would shoot anybody who crossed him without a second thought and stood in defenses of this action.

Chief Otieke was dreaded in the community. No one spent time with him. He was comfortable as a lone man. And he would stand by his decisions, though they beat hard on his family members, who nobody wanted to associate with, for fear of incurring his wrath and possibly getting shot.

His people felt very lonely and longed to associate with others. But everybody rebuffed their advances because of Chief Otieke, who never allowed his wife to complain about the mistreatment they received because of his awkward attitude towards his kinsmen and people in general.

He built a very large compound that housed his own mansion and a block of flats and rooms for tenants, including the ten-room shop complex. But he refused to give out any, indifferent to others' needs.

He had at one point rented them out in the past. However, he had used a gun to evict all the tenants one night when he had a problem of human unfaithfulness that transformed him.

Chief Otieke saw people as vampires who should not be allowed to come close to him. That way, they would not be able to devour his family members, who he cherished very much. His wife would always dispute his claimed love for them, given that he made them feel ostracized in the community.

Even some market women refused to sell to them to avoid any little thing that may degenerate into a disagreement that could mean big trouble for them. Even his shops and stalls in the market were unoccupied. He evicted the occupants and his tenants and returned everybody's full rent paid to avoid any argument that might make him pick up his gun.

He was dreaded and avoided far more than a lion. His wife had threatened on several occasions to pick up the kids and run away. And she would have done so if not for her job as a teacher in the government's secondary school in the area.

Basically, to avoid putting anybody in a difficult position, whenever she saw that a fight was brewing within him, she would leave the compound with the kids as threatened—at least temporarily.

She was a very good woman. She sympathized with others and knew how people felt about interacting with her because of her husband's strange and callous behavior. The only friend she kept begged her to keep their friendship a secret. Of course she was the one begging her friend not to leave her, so she could have at least someone to see and talk to. The friend obliged her but demanded absolute secrecy in order to avoid the wrath of Chief Otieke.

Ucheaka had only succeeded in sneaking onto the balcony to sleep during the nights because the man had removed the light bulbs to avoid giving people light. Plus, Uche always sneaked quietly, without letting anybody see him for fear of attack, although nobody stayed around chief Otieke's compound.

Anybody who had seen him sneaking in there—even the "bad actors" Uche feared might attack him—would, instead of attacking him, have cautioned him not to go there if he cherished his life. No one dared get close to that place, to say nothing of attacking anybody there. If the attackers attracted the chief, both they and their victim would be in for big trouble.

He only sneaked in to sleep there, though you could barely call his sleep-awake state restful. It was as though he was conscious of Chief Otieke on some level. Or perhaps it was the fear of the unknown that caused him to sneak, rather than going in like someone returning to his house, and remain watchful.

Ucheaka and Adanne finished eating and hung around the restaurant like many of the other people there. They watched television and waited for the night to fully fall before they would sneak into the corner where they planned to stay. At a point when they suspected that the restaurant owners had observed their state of destitution, they left and loitered, waiting for the night. As they were new to the community, they didn't know where else to go. They could have waited in the lecture room or elsewhere on campus till the appointed time, but as novices, they did not know this was an option.

"This is the first time I have been empathized with or shown mercy as a human in this place—in fact, it's possibly the first time in my entire life," Uche said as he ate. Because he had not eaten in so long, not to mention that the food was a delicacy that was, for him, a once-in-a-lifetime treat, it filled him with unimaginable satisfaction.

He ate the food because he was damn hungry and because of the love he had found for Adanne. Otherwise, he would have restrained himself, as shyness had beclouded his soul. His penury had built into him fear of getting into trouble with anyone.

"Don't mention it. You too have made me feel loved in my life, for the first time apart from my parents. Besides, the money is for both of us. The man gave it to both of us," Adanne said.

"He gave it to you, not both of us. It is your money," Ucheaka teased her.

"Okay! My money is your money," said Adanne.

As she spoke, Ucheaka again recalled his attempt at pushing her away and almost apologized. But he decided to refrain until they were in a private place. Besides, their previous discussions indicated that Adanne would not accept his apology.

"Your accommodating me today enabled me to register. Otherwise, all hopes would have been lost. Thank you very much," Adanne offered.

This statement poked at Ucheaka's peace once more, as he was brought back to the state of guilt against his action to Adanne earlier on the day. He wished she would stop this now, so that he wouldn't be compelled to apologize right there and create another scene in the restaurant. "I have heard you! Leave that for now. Let's leave here and hang around somewhere else as we wait for night. We have to be careful not to wake the owners of the compound," Ucheaka suggested, trying to stop Adanne from making statements that would indict him.

"But we are not there yet. We are still in the restaurant. Ha! How must my family be feeling now? Oh God, my mother must be half dead now for not seeing me back today," Adanne cried.

"Don't worry. Our God will communicate our good condition to them, and they will relax, okay?" Uche advised. He too thought of his family. But he swallowed his worry like a man. He saw that towing the same line of fear with Ada would nullify their good situation that God had favored them with, even if they would be staying in the open.

Adanne felt very thankful to God for having Uche, whose response to her worries suited the situation and actually alleviated her worry, preventing it from popping up again.

They paused a bit, each wondering about the kind of person the other was, reflecting on how the whole thing had come to be, and sincerely thanking God for His magnanimity.

As the night fell in full, it was finally time for them to leave. Ucheaka, who had been sleeping in the spot already, knew the right time to head there. So they retired to the balcony, with Ucheaka leading as Adanne placed her hand on his shoulder.

They needed to be very quiet and to avoid attracting any attention, just as Uche had for the past two nights. But this time, there were two people staying together. The possibility of this *not* attracting outsiders might be in doubt; honestly, it might be impossible. Nevertheless, they tried with all their wit and might to make sure they were not noticed, moving quietly and holding each other in a way that was very common among students, especially at such hours. In that way, they hoped they would not raise suspicions as Ucheaka led Adanne as though she had her sight.

They arrived at their intended destination. Looking around to be sure that nobody was peeping, as Ucheaka had done the past two days, they saw no one. They sneaked onto the balcony and sat down quietly. Leaning against the wall, they held each other like husband and wife, without any arousal but with the joy of finding each other as helper and friend.

Instead of experiencing a sensational attachment that ran down their spines, each wondered what kind of being the other, who could bring to him and to her ever-elusive luck, was. This was especially true for Ucheaka, who saw Adanne as an omen of luck, modeled to allow him to see the other side of the world. Both felt, even in the poor financial state of life they had long known, that such could never have power over them again. With the presence of each other, even their maltreatment and hunger was rendered powerless.

This feeling preoccupied them. They no longer spoke, in order not to attract the attention of the house owner. They felt more for each other as they held each other while meditating on this rare and heretofore unknown feeling of goodness that had visited them on that day. And each prayed separately in his or her heart that it would remain permanently.

Soon, they heard a strange noise. They remained quiet and became afraid that someone may have noticed them when they had entered the balcony. Ucheaka became highly jittery as he imagined what the consequence of the strange visit might be. His heart beat rapidly, he was filled with worry, he started sweating, and his breathing became uneasy.

Adanne soothed him and assured him that no problem would befall them. She touched his body and whispered in his ears that there was no need to be afraid. She assured him that the God she served, the one who had restored her lost hope in life and the one who had brought her smiles to her face again, would not leave her at the mercy of anybody. She made him understand that their coming together was for something unique that no one could, by any means, terminate.

Ucheaka was reassured and soothed by her reassurance, which made him feel as though he had just bathed with cold water, relaxed in peace, and was watching the events unfold. The two of them remained peaceful as they awaited the approach of anybody who might be coming.

Just as Ucheaka concurred with Adanne that no possible harm could come to them and that the Almighty who had performed the miracle in the registration today would save them, they saw the heavy blinding ray of a torchlight on their faces and heard a threatening thunderous voice behind the light.

Ucheaka jerked up as the light flashed in his eyes. Adanne relaxed peacefully. Though she didn't show it, she was slightly jittery; she considered that the problems she had thought to be over were evolving more and more. But her spirit assured her of God's presence, and she continued touching Ucheaka, urging him to relax.

"Who are those animals, those fools?" the unfriendly voice asked.

The steady beam of light in their eyes blinded Uche and prevented him from seeing whoever was doing the asking.

"It's us!" Ucheaka and Adanne chorused fearfully.

"Please, forgive us, sir!" called Uche. "We do not mean any harm. We just—"

"Just what, you fools?" the voice thundered.

This time, the speaker moved the torchlight from their faces, and Ucheaka saw a very huge man, with a dreadful appearance and threatening posture, gazing wickedly at them. As the man emerged from the gate of the compound, Uche saw that he held a gun in his hand. "A gun," he whispered to Adanne, and this sent the duo into a fright that nearly killed them before they could be shot. They shivered nervously.

"Who are you and what are you doing in my compound?" the man demanded. "Didn't you ask before coming here? Did someone tell you that my balcony is a chalet or a guest house?" he thundered. "You imbeciles! You came to break into my house through the shops. Your plans have failed. Your people will pick you up in pieces tomorrow."

His statement heightened the tension in the duo, who did not know what to reply. Thus far, he had not even allowed them to talk.

"I will kill you before you break into my house," the man bellowed. "I don't know who sent you, but your end is marked today, fools."

"No!" Adanne cried. "We do not have any bad intentions, sir. We are just prospective students. We finished our registration late this evening and could not go home—"

"Then you found my balcony to be a duplex . You bastards, you nitwits."

"No! Sir, we just wanted to pass the night here since we did not know anywhere else to go and then …leave …tomorrow," Uche protested, stammering nervously.

The man continued to pester them with indicting questions. But at this very moment, his wife, along with their three kids—who had overheard the interaction, especially the piteous voices of the innocent students, and knew what Chief was capable of—stormed out of the compound. The foursome had not come out to save the students, because no one interfered when Chief was unleashing his anger, but to see what was happening.

As they came out, they saw the duo writhing in fear as Chief pointed his gun at them. But they could not say a word or do anything other than watch, even against their spirits' yearnings. He tried to chase them back into the house, but they refused, saying that they wanted to watch him kill the duo.

His family became so angry that they broke his law that no one was to talk while he was talking and pleaded on behalf of the duo, whose spirits (if not their bodies) had already gone to heaven. Adanne had lost her assurance as she observed the man's hot temperament. His wife and kids, though without persuasion, pleaded with him to forgive the two students even if he wanted to send them away. They did not mind his rules but kept pleading.

But it was not in the character of Chief Otieke to forgive somebody. The family only pleaded as a formality, not hoping to achieve any result. They did so in defiance of his order that no one should talk of mercy while he was talking or unleashing terror on someone. What may have informed this rare boldness this night was only known to God.

The one spectacular but disappointing thing about Chief Otieke was that he is not illiterate. He was informed, educated not just at home, but abroad, in Britain to be precise. By this laurel of Chief Otieke, it was expected that he should correct the uninformed villagers about the advancements that had taken place in society. In fact, it might be expected that he would show them that society had graduated from the timidity that accommodated his strange attitude of callousness, moving on to embrace love and togetherness—which would be the only way for society to move forward.

But he was the one championing the attitude he should be dissuading the people from hooking onto. It was very strange to imagine that Chief Otieke was very well educated—to realize that he possessed professional qualifications that he defeated with his generally condemned character of self-isolation and gruesome treatment of whoever mistakenly tread close to him.

He was a retired public servant who had risen to high managerial position before leaving the service. But he behaved like one who came from the jungle, and this made him dreaded and avoided in the community that hosted the polytechnic.

Chief's family pitied the poor students who had fallen into his hands. And they pleaded for mercy, even though they had no recourse. They could not alter his stand or whatever decisions he may take against the duo. And they were aware that he might be very willing to include whoever tried to stop him, even though he loved them very much.

His family, especially his wife, had exhausted all her energy in trying to make Chief see how the family suffered the aftermath of his character. Even toddlers detested and spoke out against him. But his passion and extreme rashness did not allow his mind to conceive of their plight.

Being more infuriated by the family's disrespect for his rule that they should not interfere while he was dealing with his victim, he decided to involve the police. The local divisional police officer (DPO) was his personal friend. The DPO had grown tired of admonishing Chief about his behavior. He'd tried to make him understand the implications of his untoward approach to people, explaining that it may boomerang one day against him. For this reason, he should desist. However, he hadn't had much success, as Chief's mind was made up.

Nevertheless, Chief decided to call the police officer to come and pick up the duo, since his family had thrown their weight behind the pair. His family's interference had sapped him of the courage to do the two students physical harm as he evicted them. In addition, he feared that his family could be hurt while defending them, a thought that had never come to him before during his episodes of madness.

He picked up his headset to call the police, who were at his beck and call though not too willing. Adanne, seeing that he as only being selfish, called to him. Her voice radiated calm like that of an angel. Though Chief did not believe in angels anymore, her voice was very captivating and carried arresting powers.

"Chief!" Adanne called.

He did not respond. His hand remained at his ear as he waited for the line to connect him to the police station.

"Think if it were your children who were stranded somewhere where they did not know anybody this night. Think if it were them who were writhing in pains of helplessness and the harsh cold weather outside and, to worsen the already bad situation for them, somebody got them locked up in a police cell.

"Think if they were persecuted when they deserved pity. Imagine them thrown into the cold cell of the police when they should be accommodated, stripped naked in the cold when they should be clothed, and denied release even when you went for their release—all for an offence they did not commit. Think of all this happening simply because they squatted in someone's balcony, a balcony he did not use. Their only offence was their presence, as they would not take anything away from the outside of the house where they squatted, on a balcony!

"Think, Chief, if that were to happen to your children when they were beyond your presence and intervention. Think of their accusers capitalizing on their helplessness. How would you feel? How would you react?"

"I would kill the person," Chief answered without knowing that he would say so.

"Why would you kill the person? Why?" his wife furiously queried.

He stood still, as his statement had electrified him, gazing at them like a brainless man or one who had just lost his senses.

"See how it feels, Chief! I have always told you to stop this. Are you not ashamed at this question, since your children are mentioned?" his wife asked through tears.

To Chief's surprise, this voice and this question of Adanne's threw him down. He felt chilled to his spine. He had never been moved to submission like this before in his whole life.

Adanne's question was not new to him, since his wife and children had repeatedly asked him the same. But their queries had not achieved anything, as he would send them out or leave wherever they were. But coming from Adanne this night in that voice, the question seemed to have been spoken by an angel and not a human.

Chief Otieke felt a sensation in him for the first time since his life's path had changed from generosity to hostility. He couldn't control his emotions. Peace returned to his life immediately. He could not make out what was happening, but he felt like one who just passed on. He wondered what strange thing was shaping him, making him a changed man.

His life suddenly changed. He had once been a good and generous man in the community. But he'd had an experience that instantly transformed him.

The change had come after Chief had been duped by his most trusted friend. He couldn't believe it had happened. It was a massive disappointment, as his trust in this best friend of his had never wavered.

The two of them, very well known best friends, had struck a deal. They'd planned to enter into a partnership that would give them both something to fall back on after their retirement. Chief had foreseen that the deal would be a colossal one. He envisioned it helping them greatly when, soon, they were no longer receiving a salary at the end of the month nor able to access funds through imprest.

They agreed on this partnership without Chief suspecting a thing, as he trusted his friend without question. The two of them were so close they were referred to as a pair. They drew out the details concerning all aspects of the operation. His friend, who had retired before him, was to be the one running the business, while Chief would make available the working capital.

Chief, who suspected nothing, brought the cash as agreed and even some of his house documents with which they would seek a loan from the bank should the capital fall short of demand. To his incredible surprise, his friend, Chief Onyema, absconded with his family oversees with the conscious intent of duping him.

In fact, he left to go oversees to arrange for the business and never returned. What annoyed Chief Otieke most was not the absconding of Chief Onyema but the connivance with his wife. When Chief Onyema had left, his friend's wife had continued to deceive him until her papers and those of her children were ready and they joined Chief Onyema.

This incident had affected Chief Otieke emotionally and mentally and had consequently transformed him. He had become a man with a strange but monstrous nature. He had begun to hate anything going on in the name of man on earth and to abhor having anyone come close to him.

Chief Otieke had been honest while in the service. He had been a very hard-working and down-to-earth public servant. He had never believed in compromises that earned him bad remarks. He had been prudent and frugally managed his money while Chief Onyema had squandered his own with social engagements and a carefree attitude that had influenced his life negatively.

Chief Otieke had been isolated because of his stand against the evils of the day. He'd never practiced favoritism and had always wanted things done the right way—to the extent that most of his town boys who came to interviews when he was on the panel labeled him with a bad name. They were unhappy that they had failed because he had not usurped those who were rightfully successful in order to give preference to the people of his community.

Chief Otieke's real transformational problems had started when he'd discovered that his friend's treachery and that of his friend's wife, who had deceived him for months. He had fainted and had fallen into a serious coma that had lasted for days. Initially, nobody believed he would survive it. This was, in a manner, the truth. The once accommodative, generous, and tolerant man did not survive. That man was replaced by a violent beast, a circumstance no better than if he had died.

Chief would have been richer than his present financial ranking by well over 50 per cent but for the ill-fated business venture he'd entered with his friend of no measureable trust.

It would be adduced that he was mentally affected with the sudden but colossal loss of interest in anything that went by the name human or animal. He had excluded himself from the rest in the office for the remainder of the few years he served before retiring.

He withdrew his membership and participation from all clubs he belonged to and only managed to attend town meetings for the sake of his traditional bond with them. But he never participated on any day he attended, even during burials or traditional gatherings or church weddings of his people.

He had foreseen that his people might not come for his burial. Even this did not bother him, as he had already insured himself and his family. The insurance company would take care of every activity involved in his burial and handle any possible eventuality.

Even the church in which he was a knight was the first to be discarded in his life. After the betrayal, he saw every activity of the church as a ruse to deceive the unsuspecting victims. It had to be if a fellow knight could do this to him, the very same person who observed all the rituals of the church and was always applauded by the priests, who used him as a yardstick for righteousness.

The priests and church leaders had exhausted all the mapped out strategies with which to bring Chief Otieke back, including prayers. This appeared to be fueling the crisis, as the more they offered, the more Chief behaved like a deranged man.

At one point, he even used his gun to chase the reverends away, accusing them of breeding corruption in the society with the worldly interests and spiritual myopia. He demanded to know how such a person could earn all the important titles in church while the fact that he had the devouring heart of a lion went unnoticed.

Finally, society left Chief Otieke to himself as he required, no longer trying to get close to him. The only people who came close to him were the police officers he used to mistreat people in retaliation against Chief Onyema's wickedness. The officers did attend to him, but not without admonishing him on the dangers of his actions constitutionally, naturally, and traditionally. However, he never budged. He simply paid for their unruly service of manhandling his victims.

When Chief Otieke heard Adanne pose the questions, though they were not strange to him, he was reduced to a mere mortal for the first time in years. Since the business deal that had transformed him, he had only acted like a man without an end. He felt differently now. It was as if some strange thing had just been expunged from him, something that had smothered his sense of reasoning and made him act without calculating the consequences to himself and his victims, like a beast.

He realized that he had been under the influence of something. Where before he had seen beings with long tails, he now saw those around him as they truly were—fellow human beings who should be embraced. The picture of man he had previously seen deviated in every way possible from reality, causing him to detest and avoid others.

But now, he could see those people as lovable humans. This included his family members, who had not escaped his violence even though he loved them. He had never tolerated their input when it came to his actions. He had whipped and threatened to shoot them. In fact, he had made his home repulsive, despite all the worldly goods available there; many, in fact, lived in serenity without even a percentage of such natural favors.

He remained quiet. He felt like a once strong enemy caught and made a prisoner of war, as if he knew the great torture that awaited him. His silence was met with amazement by his family members, who had never—not once in the few years of his madness—seen this violent lion turn humble.

He suddenly saw himself for what he had become. He pointed his torchlight on the duo again and observed that Adanne was blind. He exclaimed, this time with a sympathetic voice and not a threatening one, "Oh! She is blind. Oh my God!"

"Yes, she is my blind sister, struggling to improve her life beyond disability," Uche replied, still jittery.

"Oh my God!" his wife cried, her voice filled with emotion. She was enraptured, especially with Ucheaka's response, and ran to meet the blind girl on the ground there, holding her as she sobbed.

He lifted her, made her sit up properly, and pulled her head to his shoulder, crying along with her while soothing her innocently.

Adanne had fallen back against the wall, shivering with fear of the possibility of persecution. But Chief Otieke's wife helped her sit up and assured her and Uche of their safety.

All the while, Chief watched them without any further words.

"Oh, my daughter, don't be afraid. My son, relax your mind," she said as she drew Ucheaka to her as if he was her biological child. "Don't be afraid. Your God is with you. We will not harm you." She cuddled their heads while her husband remained mute, wondering what was happening.

His wife had not known that he had been redeemed when she had run to hold the duo. She had risked the consequences of her forbidden action, which would have been awful had Chief still been the monster that had just been expelled from him. She held the two students, pacifying them passionately, sobbing, and assuring them of their safety. She prepared for a showdown with Chief Otieke this night.

When their three girls joined her, Chief unconsciously lit the way so they could see clearly.

"Oh! She is beautiful, mum. She will be my friend," said one of their daughters, who was also enrolling into the polytechnic this year.

"Oh yes, my angel. She is beautiful and well trained if not for her disability. But not to worry. God, who saw her this far, will finish His work of miracle on her."

They say in chorus, "Amen!"

Chief's voice could be faintly heard in the chorus.

She decided to offer the prayer again, to confirm what her ears had just heard. Chief did not chorus this time, though. She felt badly, as her joy was reduced, though she did not consider any consequence.

"You shall be my friend, you hear? Don't worry. My mum will protect you, you hear?" the daughter said, tapping Adanne, who was still not sure of her safety but reluctantly nodded her head.

"You seem to be afraid still. Don't worry. You are safe. I am here to protect you with my life. I assure you that nothing will happen to you," Ezinne, Chief's wife, said reassuringly.

Chief, whose countenance had gradually changed from unruliness to radiance, kept watching the drama with inexpressible joy. It was the first time he had experienced what could be called happiness or joy since he had recovered from his comatose condition and emerged as a violent beast.

In a twist for all those who knew Chief in that state, a louder voice thundered, "Bring them inside. They are my children. From this moment, they are part of us, members of this family. No discrimination. What we eat is what they will eat, and what we drink is what they will drink. They are gods to me. They have saved my soul from the sentence of death. I am free! I am free at last!"

Chief's statement could not be believed. His family members remained silent in confusion. They could not help but wonder if this was really happening.

But Chief keeps shouting, "Bring them inside. It is cold and unsafe here."

Ezinne jumped to her feet with a loud shout of, "Praise the Lord!"

Her words were followed by a loud chorus of "Hallelujah", with Chief's voice suppressing the others.

This made the family see that it was true—Chief Otieke had been healed by this forlorn, rejected, and despised pair.

It was within an atmosphere of sensational jubilation that Chief ordered again for the duo to be brought inside immediately.

His wife and kids led Adanne and Uche into the compound at the command of Chief Otieke. Meanwhile, he swiftly went to get the keys for his son's room. His son was studying medicine in another state at a federal university. By getting the keys, he let Adanne and Ucheaka into the company of his family, whose joy over the redemption of Chief from the clutches of death by the duo's presence in the family could not be measured.

Chief opened the door. He ushered them in, along with the rest of his family. Only his first and only son, who was away at school, wasn't there. From that moment on, his son's room became the room of the pair of students who had freed Chief from his demons.

"Look, my children!" Chief said. "From now on, this is your room until you are through with your programs. Honey, please help me tell Ibekwe, as you are going to school tomorrow, to come and take measurements for furniture for the mini-flat. We must get it ready before Chijioke returns from school in three weeks' time. That will be his apartment, as we agreed that he, as the only soon, will get married immediately upon finishing school."

The sumptuous joy in the hearts of both the family of Chief Otieke and the duo could not be quantified. All beamed with angelic smiles.

"I hereby announce that even the food you eat, as I have said earlier shall come from my pot, and your school fees shall be on my account. I shall foot all the bills you accrue. You are my children and part of this family. I am happy that my family likes you."

"My daughter," he said to Adanne, "you are sent by God for my redemption. I can't thank you enough. Your presence in my house today is a blessing. You bring a warmth and heavenly feeling that I have never had in my life. I was like one who was controlled by a vicious and evil spirit. Now I am free—I have been freed completely."

"It's night already. Let us retire to bed. And tomorrow, I shall give my testimony before you and then proceed to the church. You are an angel sent to save me, my daughter. I can't actually express my feelings here. Even if I did, no one would understand me because none of you have suffered the villainous spiritual possession or domination that I found myself in."

Chief continued to express his appreciation for the duo, especially Adanne. He spoke softly with a voice laden with emotion and sobbed soberly. His wife, who had not yet let go of Adanne, with measured appreciation, managed to leave her for a moment to go and hold her husband and her children. They all held him, patting him on the back. Eloquently, they expressed their gratitude to God Almighty, who the Chief had, only moments ago, never wanted to hear of around him.

"What kind of people are you? What special creatures are you, my children? Your coming to my house today was ordained by God and permanent. We will never be separated by man or any other force. You are gods to me. I love you! You will not leave us again. You saved my precious soul from the pit of hell. You shall always be a part of us, to nourish the good omen and good tidings you have brought to this house. You have restored here tonight joy, hope, and eternal bliss. You have done what great servants of God have tried to do but could not accomplish. Today, here and now, you have achieved just that. Oh, my children, God bless you."

Chief's statement that Adanne should remain a permanent member of the family, never to leave them again irked Ucheaka, who was filled with jealousy. In fact, he lost the joy of the moment.

He was thinking of the one thing that now most concerned him—that Adanne would be taken from him. Though he said nothing, he was filled with discomfort. His mind raged in nervousness over Adanne—the greatest blessing of his life, which God had given him, the savior of his family from the tight clutches of poverty that had held them for generations—being snatched from him just like that.

Though he managed to remain outwardly appreciative, he was writhing in pains within. He tried to interpret Chief's statement, especially after learning that Chief had a son who was almost done with his studies and who the family had decided to give a wife as soon as he returned in a few weeks.

Adanne, who intuitively sensed Uche's discomfort over the statement, tapped him as they were in each other's arms, to assure him that there was nothing to worry about. She wanted to communicate that he should relax his mind, that everything was under control, and that God was their protector.

Ucheaka was very aware of Adanne's beauty, even though she was blind, just as Chief's wife and kids were. They had all been admiring her beauty ever since they'd discovered the two of them on the open balcony. His spirit told him that Chief's son would not oblige their proposal because of her disability.

The family engaged in a very deep and passionate discussion, while the maid run about serving the duo dinner. Adanne and Uche rejected the food, claiming to have eaten. But the family insisted they at least touch the food to seal their bond of unity that God had created.

After serving the dinner, Chief and Ezinne left the room to allow the pair to eat. Two of their daughters left as well, but the one who had just registered at the polytechnic stayed with them, fondling Ada like a baby.

"Tell me about yourself. What really happened?" Chinyere asked.

The duo opened their mouths and narrated their life stories to her without mincing words. In fact, they told her everything they could remember.

She, in turn, honestly assured them of their salvation from all the maltreatments of life, as they had saved her dad. She told them that what they had achieved for the family by saving her father, who had long been the hostage of Satan, could not be quantified or fully appreciated. She also told them how her family had lived in the remotest part of hell, despite the availability of every provision life could offer. Salt, she said, had tasted bitter in their mouths until today, in this hour of God's immeasurable grace brought by them.

She assured Adanne that her brother would definitely like her, especially as she was the one who had saved the family from the mental crisis. The crisis has brought to them unimaginable skirmishes that defied all solutions. For years, the family had been unhappy, isolated, and shamefully avoided. She reported that her brother had lamented the family's troubles, saying that anybody who would save them from their quagmire of mental oppression and slavery would get whatever he or she named as the price for doing so. And she added that Adanne's payment would be marriage to Chijioke, since she was beautiful, intelligent, and spiritually gifted.

"Oh yeah! That's nice," Adanne said.

This statement of Chinyere's and Adanne's acknowledgment of the offer revisited upon Ucheaka the jealousy he had felt earlier. He felt restless and almost revealed his position in Adanne's life.

But Adanne, observing his restlessness, tapped him to cool down as she jokingly chipped in, "You should ask the boss what he thinks." She pointed at Ucheaka.

"Does he have an opinion? He is part of us too. It is a union that will go round," she said.

"I do have an opinion! My plan is to keep Adanne—" Ucheaka mistakenly started to say.

"But not for marriage. She is your sister. You should let her go and let in another you would cherish like her, who would take her place in your life with other responsibilities," Chinyere joked.

"Oh you small girl, you are well versed," Adanne said.

"Yes! Our father teaches us all things. We used to be a happy family—before his trouble, which you dealt with today."

"I see. You have gone far, baby. You are very smart," Ucheaka said.

"Like my sister-in-law here. I think I should retire to my room now. Enjoy your night, my loves," Chinyere said, bidding them goodnight.

As she left and they shut the door, Adanne and Ucheaka happily jumped onto the unique bed, a bed that they had not so much as imagined. They couldn't believe what was going on. They began to try to unravel whether they were dreaming or everything that had happened was reality. They had tried to restrain the pulsating joy, though with little success. But they had not been given a chance to talk, as Chief's family had dominated the discussion in outright expression of their immense joy.

It was another round of joy in the various rooms. All centered on the unexpected, incredible, and sudden event of the night, which had played out like a movie and had rescued the long-lost life of Chief.

Chief and his wife discussed the event in their room. The daughters of Chief discussed it in their room. And Adanne and Ucheaka did the same in their room. The daughters, whose unfathomable joy would not allow them to sleep, began a marathon list of all they can do now that their incarceration was over. They can now make friends, play with others, and satisfy their emotions. It was a large and unassuming grace that was reserved only for their family today.

Their parents discussed what kind of person Adanne could be. Chief told his wife how he had felt while in the captivity of the evil spirit. He told her how he had loathed anything that breathed, with only one thing in mind—to kill or maim. He was deeply sorry and ashamed of his behavior, especially the expulsion of the priests from his compound with a gun.

Ezinne pacified him, assuring him that everybody understood that he had not been acting normal. As such, they would not hold him guilty of his nefarious acts. She tried to make him understand that, considering what they had lost while missing him, people would rather thank God for his redemption than bring up past memories of his strange behavior.

His wife kept thanking God for bringing the strange girl with her incredible spiritual gift of healing, even in her own disability. Chief told her how he had lost control of himself while the girl spoke to him. During that moment, he had felt the sensation of angelical touch, which he had never before experienced. "She spoke ordinary words. She didn't touch me, and I was healed. I felt different and completely transformed by the time she was done with her statement. I felt relief, as though something had just been expunged from my life. I felt that my heart's heaviness had been lessened and my life had returned."

"But we have always said the exact words to you before. We have made the same statements to you in the past. Instead of accepting it, you just chased us out," Ezinne said.

"But I never heard you say such. And even if I heard, I did not understand. That is to tell you that, indeed, this girl is filled with the Holy Spirit. I truly thank God. What kind of money is it that I cannot make again? If I had been myself and cooperated with people, I would have made three times the money Onyema absconded with. In fact, I lost a lot. But I know that God will replenish it again, as I have an angel under my roof."

"I believe so. It would also be more of a blessing if Chijioke would agree to marry this girl, notwithstanding her disability. Besides, she would not go out to make money but would stay at home praying for our success. Even without sight, she sees more than one with large eyes. She is only physically disabled but is a lioness in spirit," Ezinne said.

"Honey, we need to have this girl in our house. My only fear is whether Chijioke will accept her, because honestly, if he does, I will be the happiest man. If he refuses to oblige us to marry her, then I will," Chief joked.

His wife sneered at him, tapping him jokingly and saying, "Oh yes! After all, you are a chief and a first-class one for that matter. If not for your education, you would have had two wives. But not this girl, who is like a daughter to me."

"Why not?" Chief replied, also joking.

"Chief! I hope you are not admiring this angel. Don't tell me you do."

"Why can't I admire the one who saved my life from ruin? She is my god. I have to admire her," Chief replied, continuing the joke.

"Okay, okay! But we are talking about Chijioke here and not Chief Otieke, the Ide Obodoma, the British trained economist, the husband of one loving wife whose body is gold to him," Ezinne teased, holding him firmly.

"Okay!" Chief submitted, holding her passionately and saying that, in absence of Chijioke marrying Adanne, they could give one of their daughters to Ucheaka in order to secure the relationship permanently.

"But I doubt if the duo are siblings as they claim because of the way they behave. Do not worry. Whichever way it goes, we shall be at gain as you rightly said."

"I thought as much, though that is not the issue here. Even if they are engaged, nothing is lost. We have gotten our own, which is my redemption from the clutches of the evil one who redesigned my life to a life of hostility, transforming from the compassionate, passionate, and generous man I had been known as."

"Quite correct, my darling. Chief, let's sleep. I hope to enjoy it again for the first time since you have been having your troubles. Since you changed, there has never been a time I enjoyed my sleep because of the heaviness in my heart. But now that my heart is relieved of this burden, oya, the game starts," Ezinne said, holding her husband as they fell into their bed.

"Yes, my jewel, my only jewel from heaven," Chief concurred as they retired for the sleep they wanted. They didn't get any sleep, though, due to the intrusion of unrestrained joy.

In the other room, Adanne and Ucheaka were busy with their own discussion over the day's events, especially the acceptance of and accommodation by the rich people. For once in their lives, they felt like living human beings, staying and sleeping in such a heavenly room and being treated like angels, rather than being scolded, jeered at, and mocked. They still could not believe what was going on.

"Everything is traceable to, you my dear—from the registration success to this lofty treatment. Oh God, you are indeed wonderful. Oh, Ada. I must always respect my wife, the pride of my life and the nucleus of my survival. If there shall be any, you are the boss, darling."

"Don't refer me to like that Uche. Our marriage has not even proposed. We are just friends seeking to survive together."

"Survive together, you say? What else does that entail if not unity in everything?" Ucheaka asked, beaming with affectionate smiles. He looked at Adanne, admiring her beauty. She was a sort of black beauty.

But, suddenly, his countenance changed, and he paused.

Adanne called out to him to find out what was wrong, why he was behaving strangely. "I am afraid, Adanne," he told her.

"Afraid of what? You worry too much. What is it this time?" she asked.

"I am afraid that they are about to take you, the source of my happiness in life, away from me. You are the one thing that has made me feel like a human being created by God in my twenty years in this wicked world. How can I live without you? Without you who reversed every sullenness in my life and made me escape it?" Uche replied.

"Listen to you talk," Adanne interjected angrily. "Why do you think like that? Who is taking me away from you? Can I also live happily in this world without you? Is there any better feeling one can have in this world? If there is, I don't need it and would not aspire to it. I am contented with you, so don't go there. You are not alone in your feeling. I feel the same way too."

"Okay. I am very sorry, Adanne. It's just that the way they suddenly fell in love with you is quite worrisome."

"Is that not the same way you suddenly fell in love with me? What do you people see in this poor blind girl who people have not seen in almost twenty years?" Adanne asked.

"I have told you to stop referring to yourself as blind. You are not blind as long as I am with you. Your life aligns with mine. I am your sight physically and you are my sight spiritually," he told her.

"Ucheaka, there is one more thing that I want to beg you in this relationship. If you will oblige me and keep it for me, I shall be happy and so shall you be, and our success story will never cease again."

"Amen!" Ucheaka responded and asked, "What is it that is so special to you, Ada? Even before saying it, I oblige you, unless you plan to ask me to leave your life alone. That I will not oblige. Or else I will call it quits with my life. My life cannot be meaningful without you."

"Cool down and hear me. Who is leaving you? How am I to survive without you? Stop that frightening statement," Ada cut in.

"Okay, tell me what you want."

"Ucheaka, don't tempt me. I mean don't try to make love to me before marriage. Don't take advantage of my helpless situation—"

"Shut up, Adanne. Why do you say such things to me? Taking advantage of your helpless condition. Oh no, Ada. Why do you say such a thing?"

"I am very sorry, Ucheaka. Please forgive me. I don't want to offend you. I only wanted to let you know what my God detests from me and what is the only thing that would make Him leave me. If you do it, you push away the glorious hand of God in my life, in our lives, and slay this blessing in our lives. You would, thereby, push us back to where we originated from, which would not augur well for us at all."

"Though it doesn't really surprise me to hear such things from you, as you are a very spiritual person, I must tell you that you do not deserve or need to fear any ill treatment whatsoever from me. Whatever you ask is what I must oblige, but not this. I have never thought of this in my whole life. Somebody's heart must first be at peace before being emotionally aroused. I was about to tell you this. Honestly, that's what my mouth wanted to utter before you said it. I don't have the feeling, to the extent that sometimes I wonder if I am really a man. I have never shared that with anyone except, of course, my parents. Otherwise, poverty and stigma have eroded my senses of feeling. The only thing I feel in life is pain of rejection from both God and man. I am afraid that I will find it difficult doing it even after the wedding—that my would-be wife may take me to be what I guess I am. I am like a woman. I am not aroused. I am castrated. Penury has castrated me."

"Though I understand you, I don't believe that you are castrated. It is only a thing of the mind. The mind must first be happy before other good feelings can follow. I pray very seriously that it remains as you have said until we are through with each other, so that we will not be expelled from the gracious land of God," Adanne replied.

"But these benefactors are so interested in you, my blind girl of luck. They are all over you, Ada."

"There you go again. I have told you not to worry about that. Come to think of it, how can a qualified medical doctor who has never experienced hardship in life agree to settle down with a blind girl, even if it is a smaller infirmity? Even if he agrees, we are not from the same world. We cannot suit each other. The compatibility would be wanting and never found, and that would throw us back to sorrows of maltreatment."

"But—" Ucheaka tried to cut in

"I think we should let them know of our relationship tomorrow to put a stop to all this madness of your worries," Ada said.

"No!" Ucheaka protested. "They will send us away. They kept us because of the interest they have in you."

"Did they have interest in *me* when they brought *us* in? Their interest in us is based on what God has used us to do for them this night and nothing else. Therefore, desist from such fear. We shall make them understand everything as we tell them about our lives tomorrow. They will understand, so don't be afraid," Ada assures him.

"You, you have no fear at all. You are always optimistic," Uche said.

"It is optimism that has carried me this far. I have always been positive and dogged in all my feelings and aspirations. That is why you met me here. If I had given up, I would be uselessly languishing in the corner of my village," Ada answered him.

"And I would have just been marooning the village as an object of mockery, entertaining those who feel that God only knows them," Uche added.

"Tomorrow, we will let them know that we are engaged," Adanne said.

"When did we get engaged?" Uche asked jokingly.

"In spirit, before we were born. You are asking me again. Later, you will start crying that they want to take your wife away from you. Yet, you are asking me this offensive question," Adanne joked.

"How do we go about tomorrow? Do we go to your place first and then mine?" Uche inquires.

"As husband and wife or what? How do we explain this to our parents? We are going to part ways tomorrow and go to our homes. We'll tell our parents that studies have resumed and come back in two days" time to stay together with our hosts before lectures begin. Please let us keep all these happenings secret until we are sure of their reality," Adanne suggested.

"Perfectly correct, Ada. You are quite correct. We'll go to our different places and tell them as you suggested. More importantly, we'll keep all the happenings secret from them. We'll simply tell them that we have places to stay, as we paid for it along with other fees. We'll say that we are safe and have only money issues. If what is happening here today turns out real, we shall keep everything secret and also never visit each other's places until we are ready for anything tangible; our parents would not understand," Ucheaka added.

Then they prayed and went to sleep.

The following day, they told their hosts their intention to go to their homes to see their parents, who must be worried by now. Ucheaka told them that, because he had spent three days in the community, his parents would be really worried. Adanne also said that the greatest fear her family would have was her condition, especially as she had refused their suggestion to allow her younger brother Nnachi to accompany her.

Chief Otieke's family reluctantly obliged them, after trying to persuade them to stay one more day before going. Chinyere offered to follow Adanne, but she refused. She didn't want her new friend to see her lowly place and change her parents' minds about accommodating them. Also, she wanted to keep the agreement with

Ucheaka not to share the events that had taken place with their parents.

The family of Chief Otieke bade Ada and Uche farewell and requested that they come back in two days as promised. The pair left the place, separated at the large motor garage in Ollu town, and boarded different vehicles to their home towns. As they traveled, each thought of the other, wishing they could have stayed another day, as they would have if not for concern about their parents' unavoidable worries.

On arrival at their separate homes, each was greeted without passion. Neither set of parents believed that their child had possibly been successful in the registration process. Right from the time Ada and Uche had left their homes, both of their families had been in fear, each family praying for the success of their loved one. Each family had been hoping but not quite believing that the stigma and ill luck that had long been part of their lives would not follow their loved one to finalize his or her doom, already secured in heaven.

But both families were surprised to hear the recount of success. Neither Ada nor Uche mentioned having met the other. Neither wanted to be forced into narrating with enthusiasm the good news they were yet to fully believe in. Moreover, their best reason for keeping the secret, which they had spoken of and which was spiritually bound, was to take their people by surprise.

Their people could not stop thanking God for the success, especially the acquisition of the hostel. This warded off both families' fears about the safety off their loved ones and awakened the hope that God had half woken up for them.

Mazi Udenwa, for his part, only pretended to join in the celebrations. His mind was on how this whole thing could possibly turn out successfully in the end. He was sure that Adanne's money would run out, and the family did not have any money to spend, neither to spare. He did not feel settled, as these thoughts ran wildly through his head.

Nwayimma, observing him, advised him to thank God and be hopeful. She told him that if God could help Adanne get accommodations in the hostel the first day she went to the campus, He would do the rest.

As she talked to her husband, she observed that Adanne was not wearing her glasses, which she never put down. She asked Adanne about it.

Adanne told her that the glasses had been lost on the bus she boarded. Her mother exclaimed and burst into tears.

Mazi Udenwa flared up, ranting. "Is this not what I was saying, that this school thing is just a risk?" he cried. "But you people would not listen."

His wife flared up in response, asking her husband if he was the one who had bought the glasses or had put anything into Ada's school project, beginning with her secondary school. Why, she demanded, did he always find something wrong with everything about Ada's schooling, even though he didn't contribute anything to it?

Nwayimma wondered why her husband always spoiled their good mood. They had just been thanking God for Adanne's unexpected success. And instead of joining them in thanking God, he was busy being pessimistic. She wondered what kind of man her husband was turning into.

All this while, Adanne never said a word but only mocked her father silently. She was thinking that, if all that had happened on and around the campus turned out to be true, he would be embarrassed, with God's favor. And the fears and pessimism that poverty had implanted in him would disappear like Chief Otieke's evil possessor.

Meanwhile, in Ucheaka's home, the news was greeted with joy and thankfulness to God. The family was especially grateful for his safety after three days away from the community without a trace. Their only concern was with how to get the money he would need in order to go back in two days. Uche pretended that he shared their worry, so as not to reveal the secret of Adanne yet. He only told them to only look for his transport fare to go back to school and that he would manage.

But his parents were not satisfied with his explanation. They wondered how he could manage when nobody allowed him to come close. They all left to do a large farm-clearing job that a particular chief in the village had given them. They had other jobs, which they would have done first. However, this particular chief always paid and in full. Sometimes, when he was happy, he would give them gifts as well. They decided to abandon the other jobs and work on his land first so they would be sure to get money for Ucheaka's return to school.

When the chief saw them doing the work, he was very happy. He needed it done quickly, and they had told him they would do it after completing the other work they had been given first. The chief went home; counted their money, the full money they had agreed on; and paid them in advance. Through the chief's consideration, Ucheaka's family got enough for his journey back to school in two days.

In the next two days, the duo left their homes for school as they had agreed. Upon their return to the polytechnic community, they were happily welcomed by their host family. Chief Otieke had missed them and had prayed that they would return as promised.

They hugged and exchanged pleasantries. The duo entered their room to arrange their things and then went to the sitting room to watch television, which was alien to them. They laughed and talked. Chief asked them about their people and prayed that he would see the parents of these gods one day. Everybody said, "Amen."

Adanne could not see what was going on on the television. Chinyere noticed and felt sympathetic. She took Adanne to her room while the others watched and were entertained.

Soon, Ucheaka joined them, which made Chinyere joke, "You can't stay five minutes without your angel."

He laughed and said, "Oh yes! That's true."

"One day, you people will take me to your places to see your siblings and socialize with them," Chinyere said. She wanted to see if she could love any of their male siblings as she loved Ucheaka, who was already hooked on Adanne. This did not in any way make Chinyere feel angry, however, only petty envy.

"You are very welcome, my dear. You will see them one day," Adanne said. "Maybe when they come to our matriculation."

"It will be a memorable day," Chinyere said.

"And we shall all enjoy it," Ucheaka added.

The duo and the family lived together happily. Chief Otieke reintegrated into the community with a sumptuous thanksgiving that attracted all from near and far.

It was a very great occasion that the community would not soon forget. He introduced the "adopted" duo as the tools God had used to do His great work—a worked that that eluded all those who had tried their best to intervene in the past. Chief apologized to everyone he had offended while under the captivity of Satan and announced his forgiveness of Chief Onyema's betrayal, wishing his old friend good luck wherever he was.

The *igwe* of the community thanked the duo and promised them both safety and citizenship within the community. He promised Ucheaka a chieftaincy title once he graduated and got married, since the title was not given to an unmarried man. The igwe told them that they would be crowned as soon as they got married, which made Chief Otieke and his family happy, even though Chief Otieke regretted not being able to make his relationship with the duo permanent through marriage.

He now knew, given everything he'd learned about the duo, that neither could marry into the family. But he held out hope that one of the duo's siblings might be suitable for marriage to one of his children. But the problem was that their siblings were stark illiterates who had not gone to enough school.

Adanne's siblings were better off, as they had managed to attend some school. Ucheaka's siblings, on the other hand, did not go to school as a result of the poverty that had hold of the family.

Chapter Four

The Conglomeration

Having lost the hope of permanently sealing their relationship with the duo, Chief Otieke and his wife started thinking of setting up a business for the Ada and Uche in the unoccupied shops in the strategic corners of the polytechnic community.

Having seen the spiritual attachment in their lives and what God could do with their lives, Chief and Ezinne felt that it was best for them to set up a business for their adopted children to combine with their studies. Since they were both brilliant, they would not be distracted or frustrated.

They believed quite optimistically that the setup would definitely help the duo, as well as helping them to recover the losses they had incurred as a result of Chief Onyema's betrayal. Believing in God's grace in the duo's lives, they thought it wise to do so; it would be the best reward they could give them. Adanne and Ucheaka, meanwhile, could not even imagine that the family might be hatching such a huge plan for them. They only casually hoped for a good plan that would bring about the changes they needed.

Chief and Ezinne decided on a provision shop. In the meantime, people started rushing to rent the other shops, after seeing Chief Otieke's return to normalcy. But he politely turned down the offers. He hoped to give the duo one of the shops and then think of what to do with the rest. After he had pondered the options, he would give the remaining shops out if he had not come up with a better suggestion.

The family called Ada and Uche one night after dinner to announce the new plan, which they joyously accepted. They told the family that they too had been thinking of a similar setup, so that they could contribute to the feeding of the household. To God be the glory that Chief was thinking the exact same thing.

Chief dismissed the idea of them using the shop to contribute to the feeding of the family. But he aligned with their joy, which could see no bounds. He was very happy to be in a business partnership with the duo, whose relationship he saw as a blessing already.

A few days later, Chief set the duo up with man in the corner of the community who had experience in the type of business Ada and Uche would be running. The man would train them on the nitty-gritty details of the business. He had tried to rent shops from Chief both during and after the madness, but Chief had refused. Initially, the man objected on the grounds that Chief refused to give him a shop. But Chief opted to pay him for his services. The man agreed to collect the wages offered but continued to insist that Chief should give him a shop from his line of shops. Nevertheless, Chief declined.

After the training, Chief gave Ada and Uche money to go on their first voyage. They did so, starting with one of the shops. In addition, they attended their lectures diligently.

All of this they did without any hitches, which was the result of a combination of two things. First, Ada and Uche were not frustrated or distracted by the business, as by handling it, their brilliance was not in any way tampered with. Second, they still measured up in their studies.

Their business grew immeasurably. In fact, it grew in geometric proportions. It was as if the wares on the counter increased overnight. Even they were surprised.

This unprecedented and rapid growth marveled everybody. Chief could not hide his joy. His dream of helping to lift the duo who had saved him out of their poverty-stricken living conditions were coming true, not to mention that he no longer thought of Chief Onyema's betrayal.

What of the duo? Both Ada and Uche were incredibly joyous over the gradual exit from their previously forlorn lives, the lives in which their families lived that did not seem like the life intended for human beings created by God. They were also so pleased with their coming together that a song and recitation that never got monotonous in their mouths was constantly on their tongues.

The shop became the last bus stop for the students and staff of the school. It was so popular that whoever had not gone there to get the supplies he or she needed would find his or her stuff (purchased elsewhere) viewed as fake. The business boomed, and the shop hummed with customers. All of this held everybody spellbound.

Suddenly the business bloomed into a big supermarket and could no longer contain enough wares to meet customers' needs, even though they used some unoccupied shops in Chief's compound to store their goods. Seeing this tremendous development, Chief decided to give them the remaining shops, which he had refused to give out even after his recovery. The walls between the stores were broken in order to transform the store into it a full large supermarket.

Adanne and Ucheaka employed attendants who worked in the supermarket. They hired very active boys and girls and paid them a good salary to ward off any thought of dishonesty. All of the employees served diligently after hearing the story of the duo. They all feared that the duo would learn of any hanky-panky played by anyone. And even if the two didn't know, their God would definitely expose the person.

One night after dinner, Adanne and Ucheaka, who had totally changed and had a come to embody all the beautiful features God had made them with, approached Chief Otieke and his family in the sitting room.

By now, Chief's son had returned. He was very interested in Ada, whose beauty was captivating, apart from the sight problem. But he had been made to understand that the duo was engaged. This really beat him down.

He was doing his residency at a nearby hospital. Thus, he lived at home. He always hung around the duo wherever they were—at the shop or in their room or anywhere else they went—apart from when they attended lectures. He ate from their pot, which was an extension of Chief's family pot.

The duo entered the house with a bottle of expensive British whiskey that Chief liked drinking and asked for everybody to be around. Chief had been with his wife before they entered, and two of the daughters had been waiting for their NYSC (National Youth Service Corps) posting. The other two—that is the son and youngest daughter—were called in.

When they arrived, Uche began, "Daddy, Mommy, my brother and sisters here, we are here to thank you for the unimaginable thing you have done in our lives. You have transformed our lives from the perpetual bondage of hopelessness to something people admire and try to emulate today—"

"No!" Chief protested. "Don't say that, my children. Don't say that. We should be the ones thanking you. Do you know what you did for us? What have we done for you that is greater than saving me from the pit of hell and, today, supporting me like biological children? Oh, no! My children, don't mention it."

"Daddy is right, my children. You don't need to do what you are doing now. We all understand how it all started and cannot deny the fact that you are angels with us," Ezinne said.

"Everybody is correct. My daddy here has played a role in Ada and Uche's lives, and they first played a role in our daddy's life. That cannot be denied. There must always be gratefulness to make the world move on with more generosities. Let's hear them, Dad," Dr. Obinna said.

"You are right, Doc. We are not kids, and we know why we are here, even though your response is quite astonishing and makes us blush. We really understand, Daddy, Mommy. But allow us to appreciate you please," Ucheaka pleaded.

"Okay, my children, go on. I am all ears. It's just that I find it difficult to see you appreciating me when I should be the one appreciating you," Chief said obliging as best he could.

"Daddy! I must say thank you first, before telling you that we are here to …to …" Ucheaka stammered, adding, "You have made me feel a bit shy. But anyhow, Daddy, from the look of things, you would agree with me that we are rapidly progressing in the business you set up for us and that it is not having any adverse effects on our studies.

"From the day we entered your house, you called us your children, promising that there would be no discrimination. We eat what you eat and drink what you drink. And since then, it has been like that. You have not reneged on your promise. The love increases by the day, rather than lessening. No discrimination has been observed in any small way.

"Now I want to ask you people a question, Daddy and Mommy."

Chief felt taken aback as he wondered what the question might be. As did Ezinne, who could not control her fears. "Have we offended you?" she asked.

"No, Mommy. Offence has no place in this discussion," Ucheaka replied.

"Then what is it? You have never acted this way before, rising to question us, since we have been living together. What could be the matter, my children?" Chief submitted, waiting for an answer.

"Okay! To douse the tension and lessen the curiosity, I shall go straight to the point now."

"Please do. We are kept in suspense. Please do tell us your mission," Chief worriedly replied, looking nervous.

"Daddy and Mommy, my question is, why do parents train their children or prepare them for a better life ahead?" Ucheaka asked.

"Have you not been taking care of your parents all this while? I was even thinking of coming to meet you two to ask about them," Ezinne questioned.

"Far from that, Mommy. Far from that. Just answer the question—our question, mine and Adanne's question."

"Okay." Chief cleared his throat and adjusted himself in his seat. "The real reason parents struggle hard to give their children a better place in the future is that they should, in turn, be taken care of in their time of dependency, just as Lolo alluded to in her question to you."

"Chief, you are our parents, and you have given us a future that cannot be closed in life again."

"Amen!" everybody chorused.

"And this is your time of dependency. You have done your part, and it is now the children's turn to do their part. I want to present you this drink and announce that, from this very moment, the family, Chief Otieke's family will be dependent on Uche and Ada's supermarket. Anything called a bill to pay—the food, the water, and even the air the family breathes, if it is bought—will be shouldered by us, all of us, the Uche Ada Supermarket.

"Chief and Mummy, you should go on retirement finally. You must relax and enjoy the fruits of your labor, while the responsibility of the children falls on us. Also, Doc, you should start thinking of what you want to do after your residency. In fact, we are capable of doing everything. I also want to announce that the name of this supermarket will be changed from Uche Ada to something that will include this family, and the supermarket will be registered as jointly owned. We are expanding. God is blessing us. We have acquired shops in the neighboring communities. We shall move in next week. We just wanted to surprise you.

"The next plan is to extend to townships, which shall be in effect very soon. Chief and Mummy, you are the gods. God brought us together for a purpose, to make Chief forget Chief Onyema and still reach his aspirations. More importantly, Chief Onyema was used for us to come together. We should know that."

Chief fell back on his chair, shouting, "Another angelic voice, another recovery—first from the devil's captivity and now from dwindling financial strength that wants to imprison me again after the devil left me."

Shouts of joy and merriment were shared around the room as everybody hugged each other, and the atmosphere was charged with celebration galore. Nobody said anything. Rather, all shared overwhelmed smiles and loud and joyous laughter. Shouts of, "Praise the Lord," rent the air.

Of course, everybody lacked words to express their joy. It was like the saying that, if a woman is given fat meat to prepare soup, her joy will not allow her to blow the fire. The joy in her heart would prevent her mouth from blowing the air necessary to light the fire.

Chief could only shout, "Is this a dream? Who are these people? Are they humans? How did this happen? The boy and girl I wanted to lock up have turned out to be the pair upon whom my life will depend. What a world of irony!"

Ezinne, for her part, could not open her mouth to talk at all.

The doc was overwhelmed with amazement. The overseas journey he had hoped to plan after completing his residency had become a reality, and he has been worried about the possibility due to financial issues. The daughters went and held Adanne, cuddling her and calling her an angel in disguise.

Chief Otieke had actually made money during his service years—real honest money. But his financial status had dwindled frantically, largely due to Chief Onyema's theft of a large chunk of his money.

He had since been spending the large savings he'd made and the retirement benefit he was paid, with no means of replenishment. He had driven the tenants out of his houses, stalls, and shops and so had lost any income from that avenue.

Because of this financial approach, he had faced rapid depletion of his treasury. This was so much the case that his son's request to travel overseas to practice after acquiring his professional certificate was like a swarm of bees, even as he pretentiously obliged him, complaining all the while about financing the voyage. The very ugly face-off about the inadequacy of his father's financial resources to sponsor the trip had affected Obinna emotionally. He couldn't stop thinking about the fact that the cause of the situation was his father's madness. For as a part of that madness, Chief Otieke had rebuffed every business opportunity that had shown up.

But today, this hour, the work of the Lord had sent the duo, Ucheaka and Adanne, to care for the family as Uche had just promised they would. Seeing the redemption of his father as a preamble, Obinna was elated at the prospect of the uninhibited fulfillment of his heart's desire—a desire that had been threatened by his father's rapidly dwindling financial strength.

His joy outdid that of the others. Among the rest, though, one could not determine whose happiness outweighed the other.

Everybody was reduced to unrestrained childish joy. They would have refrained from the impulse or reduced the flame from flaring so high, had they been conscious that the joy had been sapped.

The business kept growing at a rapid pace that the trio could hardly understand. They branded the supermarket chain with a new name— Otucheada Supermarket—to include Chief's family as a bona fide part owner of the property. The agreement was not to share profits. Rather, it placed everybody on a monthly salary. Their respective family welfare was taken care of through the business, without concern about the magnitude of the demand from anyone in the family. They now operated as one family.

Meanwhile, Adanne and Uche sent only peanuts to their parents, with the guise that they had been able to secure teaching jobs in the community, preparing students for O level, JAMB, and other examinations. This was a secret that only the duo knew. They kept it to themselves, as they knew Chief and Lolo would not support it. But they did this because they planned to take their people by surprise.

Their parents were enthusiastically and boundlessly happy. Their children, whose relationship had not been revealed to them, had been so graced by God's favor that they could now take care of themselves, without demanding anything from them, and could even send them peanuts.

Changes occurred in their respective homes, though none were tremendous. After all, the duo only sent a meager upkeep, even as they were swimming in an ocean of ceaselessly flowing cash.

However, both sets of parents became constantly in doubt of what their child related about his or her position. The new appearance of the duo was enough to cast doubt. Though neither ever wore gorgeous clothes when they visited home or allowed any accompanying signs of their financial favor to follow them, their bodies could not deny the reality. Ada's beauty and Uche's handsomeness, once underground, buried by the harshness of unrelenting poverty, had fully remerged. Both were filled with great joy. Their families did not fail to pester them with questions, attempting to know the true position of things.

As the duo continued to claim that it was just the teaching appointment that made them joyous and prosperous, their parents returned to gratefulness to God for His favor. Each set of parents accepted what their child claimed, which to them had little meaning, other than that progress was being made—progress that might give their lives a face-lift.

Adanne, who had acquired a pair of better-quality eyeglasses, asked her parents to help her thank God for making it possible for her to get them with her first three months' salary. However, her mother had gone with her when she had purchased the first pair of glasses, which was inferior to this new pair. She knew what the glasses must certainly cost. And she also knew it was doubtful that the salary Ada would be earning with a part-time teaching job could cover the cost of these quality glasses.

Everything changed, though not remarkably, for the families of the duo with the stipend each sent his or her respective family. Ada and Uche kept this up in order to keep the whole affair to themselves, planning to disclose all to their families in due time.

The business grew from a supermarket to a full commercial business venture that spanned across the country. Chief Otieke's family's needs were met in full by the venture. Chief would repeatedly query Ada and Uche on the welfare of their respective families. The pair would falsely assure him that their families were all right and that they would soon come to thank them.

At one time, Chief opted to go and see their families to ascertain the level of care they receive, but Ada and Uche both refused. At Chief's insistence—they could no longer argue, as they didn't argue with his decisions—they revealed to him how meagerly they had cared for their families. They explained that they didn't want their families to know of their relationship and that they wanted to take them by joyful surprise when the time was right.

They convinced Chief that this was their decision. Though he did not doubt them, he was not comfortable with the situation. Chief worried about the suffering that still went on in the families, whose children were already millionaires. He decided to force Ada and Uche to tie the matrimonial knot now, to release their waiting joy and comfort.

They agreed with him, though without telling him that they wanted to marry when they were through with their National Diploma (ND) program.

"But these people are suffering, and God has blessed you to change their story. Why keep it a secret? I am not a part of this, my children. Let's make it now. My family cannot enjoy it alone. Please."

Ada and Uche reasoned with Chief and agreed to make this change soon. But Chief objected to the notion of "soon," saying that it had to be now. At last, they agreed without further argument.

Though still in the first year, to sum it up, the business had squarely triumphed. The stores in the polytechnic community had become the center of shopping for students and lecturers alike. All were very eager to buy from them because of the relatively cheap prices and the resounding love for the duo, even though many facilities to entertain customers were available.

The store employees barely had time to catch their breath, as they were constantly engaged in attending to the customers almost twenty-four hours a day. Some of the lecturers shopped and paid at the end of the month, and even some students were on such a plan. It was a privilege that Ada and Uche gave out to compensate for the difficulties those who lived lives of abject poverty faced. This way, they were able to help some students whose circumstances were like their own, though not in the same magnitude (as none could compare). They knew what it was like to never have sympathy, even from others who were also forlorn.

Chief Otieke, who could not hide his ecstasy about being a principal partner in the business, decided to manage the branch in front of his house. That way, he would keep himself busy on paid service. This was something he wanted to do even though the family's bills were settled by the fast-growing business.

Everything was settled, and God's favor was clearly and constantly visible. The venture had grown. Uche Ada was no longer a one-building supermarket. It had transformed into Otucheada Supermarkets, a business empire with branches in various parts across the country. And each of these branches were succeeding as rapidly as had the first store due to the honesty with which the attendants offered their services.

Uche and Adanne resisted Chief Otieke's request to manage the business near his home. But he insisted, on the premise that, if he remained inactive, he might fall sick as an old man of nearly seventy years.

Adanne and Ucheaka became the subject of the community's discussion, admiration, and emulation. Those who had seen the pair struggle and had seen Adanne's grip on Ucheaka on registration day did not believe what they were seeing. They were now in the best place to narrate the genesis of the spontaneous change of life for the very best.

Those registration officers who had considered the duo on that day were not left out in the doling out of favors the business was known for. They did their shopping almost without pay, especially the man who had given Adanne money. He would now blush when he came to the shop. Each time, he would hear the same statement, "The boss has paid." And he would always feel abashed, especially recalling the treatment he and the other registration officers had given the prospective students that day. He pinched himself after asking if he could borrow money from them but got a grant and then at loan.

Don't despise anyone, no matter the size of his or her disability; for God's grace does not know disability, much less measure it, he told himself.

Even though the expansion was quite observable in all spheres, Ada and Uche were still struggling to firmly reach their lofty goals. Their target was reaching the conglomerate level. They were on their way, having established the rudiments of thriving fortunes to come, and intended to press forward. After all, they would say, opportunity comes but once.

They decided to go ahead and formalize their relationship into marriage. Thus, they would bail out their families, who had been victims of their secrecy. They would enable their families to enjoy the great grace that God had showered on His forlorn children.

Initially, they'd planned to marry after their graduation, which was another few months away. But they saw how their secret had denied them the opportunity to share what God had brought to their families. They didn't believe that the favor was specifically for them alone; rather, they believed that it was meant for their entire families, who had never really had the true taste of salt in their lives.

In addition, Chief and Lolo Otieke's relentless persuasion influenced their decision. Chief and his wife were constantly threatening to find the way to their homes to bless the families that had produced their saviors. They didn't want the surprise they had planned for their families to be exposed ahead of time, which might be the case, considering Chief's stern position on the matter.

Furthermore, they were finding it difficult to resist the emotional feelings that were threatening them. They decided to do it and feel each other for once. They could hardly resist anymore.

Adanne, who knew the consequences of doing this before marriage—not only a loss of favor with God but also a sentencing of her soul to hell by Satan (consequences she could hardly forget and would never forgive herself for incurring)—had firmly proposed the idea. Her proposal was met not with Ucheaka's dispassionate support, but with his eagerness. He had attempted their premature union on several nights. On each occasion, his desire had been denounced by Adanne's voice of caution, which brainwashed him like Chief Otieke's own, and he would lose his erection instantly and passionately apologize. Adanne would not hold him guilty, seeing the impossibility of the stimulation they stirred in one another.

They fixed the date during the vacation of the first semester, year two. Chief and Lolo offered to go with them. However, they did not oblige the offer, on the grounds that they wanted to really surprise their people. They wanted to create for their families a day that would forever remain memorable in their lives.

They informed Chief of their decision to build some small good houses for their families. Doing so would buttress their claim that God had granted sumptuous favor on their families, who would not believe so easily. Their families had long since given in and accepted their lot of poverty. They had closed their minds to the possibility that people's situation in life may be dynamic, at least as far as they were concerned in this wicked world.

Chief objected to the suggestion of small houses. He suggested instead building edifices befitting the great things the Lord had done in their lives. However, they made Chief understand the philosophy that guided their decision: "Gradualism is an approach to life that nets a permanence to living in gain." The business, they pointed out, was still growing and could not shoulder such houses as those of his imagination.

Chief still objected, saying that the pair had done enough for his family and should do the same for their families now. The duo, in their unwavering wits, convinced Chief to compromise. They would slightly expand the architectural design of the houses they were envisioning for their families, but they would not build palatial homes.

Chief Otieke suggested that they take a car to share the news with their families. But Ucheaka bluntly refused the offer, for reasons he did not disclose to anybody at this time.

Ostensibly, he wanted to see the reaction of the family to Adanne's condition, though it was not very apparent at present because of the high-quality eyeglass she had procured. This improvement had come despite the fact that the only solution to her disability was to kill the snake and prepare food from its meat for her to eat—an aspiration that was now unattainable. No one had been able to find the snake after all this time. Of course, nobody would think that the snake could still be alive. At had been almost nine years since the incident. That the snake had likely been killed somewhere remained the reasonable assumption.

After all the suggestions and objections, Chief, who respected Ada and Uche's opinions like those of the spirits, had been shrugged into submission. He would allow them to do this their way. He did wish they had accepted his offer, but he did not regret anything. He knew that they must have cogent reasons for their plans, which he believed would play out better in the end.

The duo waited impatiently for the day on which they would go home. It reminded Adanne of waiting for school to resume so she could go back to basic six.

And the day that had drawn near so stealthily, crawling like a new baby into the wind of their anxiety, finally came at last. Despite its refusal to arrive quickly, the sun kept giving way to night and reappearing for the day, and each new day was recorded, until their sum brought about the anticipated day. Adanne and Ucheaka left, boarding a chartered vehicle straight to Ucheaka's house. Their arms were loaded with gifts, especially foodstuff and clothing. They felt as they had on that first day, on that very hour when they had walked side by side to the gate after their registration, a sensation they could never forget and recalled so often.

They beamed with smiles previously unmatched, especially as the sacred apple would be touched in less than forty-eight hours, for the first time in almost twenty-three years on earth.

They joked with each other, to the amazement of the driver, who had heard about the duo but didn't know it was them who were his passengers. Nevertheless, this interaction stuck in his mind. He saw the couple play and joke. One could hardly observe Adanne's blindness when she as with her heartthrob, who, of course, she never walked without.

As they arrived at Ucheaka's compound, they met everybody as though the arrival had been scheduled. Ordinarily, the family would have been on someone's farm working. But by providence they had not gone out on that day. Their daily labor routine was no longer as demanding. The stipend Uche sent had solved many of their financial issues and had reduced the amount of time they needed to spend laboring on other people's farms.

His parents and siblings stormed out in fear of hearing a cab enter their place for the first time. They were engulfed with the fear that harm may have come to Ucheaka, the only hope of the house. They reasoned, though, that even if something had happen to him, he wouldn't be brought in a car, considering his lowly position in life.

They stood there, shivering and waiting for the real event to unfold, only to see Ucheaka alight from the cab, strong and hearty and beaming with a joyous smile. The first fear was that he had come for money, forgetting that he was the one sending money.

As his people say, "When the mind of a man thinks too deeply into a problem, he mistakenly greets the sheep." Having been made slaves by striking poverty, the family could not help that their minds went first to financial requests that could not be granted.

As Ucheaka observed their fear, he calmed them down, telling them to chill and come home from their thoughts. He assured them that he had not returned to collect money from them but to leave money with them. They immediately regained their consciousness and ran to hug him. It was an exaggerated jubilation over having a vehicle come to their place for the first time in their lives. His younger siblings ran to touch the cab with admiration.

But as Adanne stepped out of the cab and greeted them, their countenances changed. They cleaned their faces to clearly see what was going on. Adanne and Ucheaka observed this reaction but were not bothered. It was what they expected of it and possibly the reason they had kept their secret for so long.

The atmosphere of gaiety waned. In fact, it subsided spontaneously, even as the younger ones reluctantly offloaded the foodstuff and clothes from the cab. His parents pretended to be happy and welcomed the girl. Then they watched the children carry the gifts inside, a situation that would have driven them mad with giddiness, if not for Adanne's intrusion.

Yes, Adanne to them was the obstacle to their fully luxuriating in the great feelings they believed they would have otherwise been experiencing for the first time in life. They would have probably rolled over each other in celebration of the unimaginable changes in the circumstances of their family life Uche's gifts signified. However, the sight and presence of Adanne spoiled the great Display of God's true interest in Mazi Obilo's family, who had suffered undue deprivation for decades.

Why the bad omen? Why this joy spoiler, this happiness drainer? Why? These were the confusing thoughts going on in the minds of each of Ucheaka's family members. The children did seem to be less burdened with these thoughts, as they were busy unloading the cab. They carted into the house items that seemed to have sworn never to enter the family abode. And because of their unwavering discrimination against the family, these items were swiftly packed into the house, before they could start running away from the family that was like a taboo to them.

As Uche's siblings busily moved the items in, their parents beamed with smiles of admiration. Finally, their fortunes had arrived. This they saw, despite the seeming stain of Ucheaka bringing a blind girl home.

Ucheaka led Adanne inside the hut, beaming with the smile that had eluded, in fact avoided, the family for decades. Adanne reciprocated that smile, showing all her angelic beauty. And this infuriated Ucheaka's parents all the more.

Their ire was suppressed by the amazement of the unusual tidings that paraded into their lowly holdings, which the cab could not enter fully because of the narrowness of the path that led to their home. After all, no vehicle ever came here. Still, the Obilos managed to ask themselves about the sanity of Ucheaka in this foolhardy action of his, especially now that God had smiled upon them.

They became disturbed over this unimaginable development now that God had blessed them. God had taken away from them the reproach of wretchedness, only for Ucheaka to replace it with that of defamation. They saw her condition as more repressing than that of dehumanizing poverty. Because of having been subjected to the latter, they remained quite unaware of the true reality of the development.

Ucheaka had changed a lot, as had Adanne. The features of his once imprisoned handsomeness were conspicuous, as though to announce their defeat of the jailer. His parents noticed this and felt even more aglow as they took in his appearance along with the dreamlike events of this morning.

Ucheaka had had a lot of temptations from campus girls, who flood after him. They were attracted to his brilliance, along with his impressive physique and wealth. But he and Adanne had remained inseparable, a togetherness bridged only by the time they received lectures in their different departments.

These girls, who were not privy to the genesis of Ada and Uche's union fumed at his easy dismissal of their advances. He declined even to assist anyone in her academic work, in order to start resisting the devil from the bud. He believed that allowing any of the girls to come close could trigger unsolicited feelings to which he might possibly yield. Consequentially, he would lose the Lord's interest in him, which was only sustained by his relationship with Adanne; or rather, it was sustained in Adanne.

Some of the girls, even after becoming fully aware of the genesis of his relationship with Adanne and their wealth, still wondered why he played the fool by clinging on to the blind girl, even after making it. One girl openly mocked him one day after he rebuffed her request to assist her and her friend in a course they found difficult. In truth, they hoped to win Uche's affection and steal him from the blessing that was Adanne, whose place in his heart they sought to usurp.

She told him that he was simply handsome and rich for nothing, since he still had an empty brain. She insulted him, saying that the poverty he'd once endured had seriously affected his brain adversely. Otherwise, why wouldn't he push the poor blind girl away and live the life he seemed to deserve—the life God had given to him.

This statement had hit Ucheaka hard. He'd recalled the same pressure to push Adanne out on that fateful blessed day of no small import. He had wept silently as he'd remembered how he had almost yielded to that pressure—a pressure that had only one mission, which was to deny him this day and the wonderful circumstances he found himself in. Thus, his love had become all the more rooted in Adanne than ever. From that point on, he'd had Adanne sit on his lap anytime, anywhere, and on every occasion. He didn't do this to attract jealousy but to portray their inseparability and to be clear that there was no vacancy in his life, because Ada had filled it.

The Obilos, though inexpressibly joyous, felt the intruding sentiment of misgiving. They nonetheless allowed the duo to get settled down before opening the cankerworm of queries they had lined up for Uche.

As the siblings finished emptying the cab of the contents that Ucheaka had brought home, they saw their parents standing in a defiant posture. They watched Ucheaka lead Adanne into the hut.

The smaller one, Chika, went to hold Ucheaka's hand as he entered the hut with Adanne. There started the catalogue of queries separately arranged by each of Uche's family members. Ucheaka was fully ready with answers to each of them.

"Brother! What is wrong with Aunty? She gropes, doesn't she see?" Chika asked as her mother fumed and shrugged in objection.

"Oh, Chika, my dear. Aunty is all right. She sees even you who are here," Ucheaka replied, pointing to his sister's heart.

Adanne called to her. "Chika."

"Aunty!" she answered.

"You shall be my friend, okay. I shall give you gifts, you hear."

Chika then replied, "Brother, I like Aunty. I will be her friend. She is beautiful."

She would have continued, but her mother shut her up, to Ucheaka's displeasure. "Shut your mouth, you parrot. It is all these items Ucheaka brought home that are intoxicating you," his mother told Chika.

"She is not a parrot, Mother. She speaks the truth. She sees the truth you may not be seeing. But the little girl sees," Ucheaka said in a hot but gentle voice.

"Ucheaka! Don't be harsh. Remember, we expected this that—"

"Its okay, Ada. I understand," he cut in, cuddling her with fondness.

Adanne kept quiet, not saying another word. She wasn't bothered or upset by this little display of dislike, as Uche's family was ignorant about the whole success story. She held the unbiased belief that they would nearly mob her once they came to know the truth surrounding her steadfast relationship with Ucheaka and how it was what had just now filled the house with goodies that it had heretofore never seen.

Ucheaka led Adanne the rest of the way into the hut and had her sit down on the wood piece they used as chair. They had no extras, since nobody ever visited. Meanwhile, his parents retired to the back of the house, putting a little distance between themselves and Adanne, so she would not overhear them. They began to quarrel about the situation, which they could neither believe no understand, no matter how clearly it was explained.

They then sent for Ucheaka to come and talk with them. But just as his sibling was about to go get him, Ucheaka, who had been coming to meet them, approached. He was beaming with a smile that was impossible to resist and that showed that nothing was wrong. This hit his parents hard. They began to become concern about his mental stability.

He joyously called, "Mama, Papa, I know you are wrestling seriously in your minds. Chill out; calm down. The tidings I bring will make you doubt whether you are still yourselves and in this world".

"What good tidings? Tidings of leading a blind girl home? Or what, I wonder, might be other good tidings you have for us?" his mother raved.

"At least the tidings of having rice in a bag for the first time in your lifetime and of not being able to eat only once in two years—provided, that is, that those villagers of ours give you what they owe you after you've cultivated their farms," Ucheaka joyously joked. He could not stop smiling broadly .

"Ucheaka, please come close. As you can see, we sent Omume to come and call you before you coincidentally came," his father said.

"Yes, Father, Mother, I am here now. Talk; my ears are wide open," he says, holding the two of them together in his two hands.

"Ucheaka, my son, what is this you are doing? Are you all right? Who is that blind girl with you? Though you have not said anything, we can guess what is in your mind. Yet, we want to hear it from you. Who is she? What is she doing in your life?" his father thundered.

"But, Papa." Uche leaned in closer. "But, Papa—"

"We don't want to hear any reason whatsoever you are thinking of her," his father interrupted. "Do you want to bring shame to this house? We are worth nothing out there, jeered and mocked like people whose life is not owned by God's presence. We manage and endure. Now that God wants to think of whether to think of us or not, you are bringing this disgrace to us."

"And the worst of it is that it doesn't move you. You have already been bewitched. You don't seem to understand the implication of your action," his mother added, trying to sob.

"Ucheakachukwu! Why! Why? This is quite absurd. The people will despise us the more. How can we be consciously retrogressing? How can we bring worse pain—pain inflicted by ourselves? We should be thinking of thanking God now that He has, for once in almost a century, thought of us. But see us, instead, demeaning the good grace He has splashed at us. We can now think of eating such foods we have never before enjoyed—a thing we should have done with joy. But you are trying to mix this new food with grains of sand. Why? My son! Why?" his father demanded still fuming.

Uche snorted, looking down with his eyes fixed on his parents as they blabbed. He did not, however, take offence at their words, as they were ignorant. He only felt a heavy disappointment that, despite all he had brought home—a bounty that should have elicited their joy—they were allowing such unwarranted emotion to override the joy. Still, he tried his best to keep his peace, consoling himself with the reminder that their ignorance of the whole story was a part of their mismanagement of their feelings.

"Mother, Father, thank you so much for your concern for me, which is never in doubt and which has been constant from my birth, as well as that of my siblings. But I want you to know that your son, of whom you are proud, has never changed. If at all any change has occurred, which is evident today, it is for our own good, our most unexpected betterment.

"My responsibility is to give this house a future. I will take us away from the caricature the entire village has made it to be, even though we ask nothing from anyone, apart from the ability to work their farmland, for which they do not even pay fairly.

"I cannot be so selfish as to find joy in a blind girl, a true joy, and enjoy it alone without your participation. Everything I do is for the good of this family—"

"Not marrying a blind girl," his mother cut in.

"Allow me to finish, Mother. Just allow me that. You won't understand now. But I strongly believe you will when the whole scenario is laid bare to you in order to remove the log in your eyes. But if I may ask, with apologies, do you care about me really as you claim?"

"Of course, we do. You know that. If we did not, would we be concerned about the mistake you are about to make?" his mother replied, though mildly.

"Are you beginning to doubt us, my son, just because we want to correct you? Don't you know that you are trying to bring more penury as we are about to exit the curse that this life has been?"

"More penury, you say, Father! Well, we have permanently exited penury, never to perceive the smell in this house again. Just relax and tow along with me, your trusted son, who is an ally with you in this loathed life of dearth we are about. In fact, we have just bid such a life goodbye forever."

"Ucheaka! Are you sure all is well? The way you sound makes us fall deeper into our fears," his father said, frowning. "The question is, have you suddenly started to doubt us or stopped being concerned for your welfare, your future, and the good of our family?"

"No, not at all. I have not and will never doubt you, my parents. I would not even imagine such a thing. But if I may ask again, if you truly care about me, can you consider practically the changes in this house today? Can you at least consider my demeanor before you today and appreciate and applaud me with admirable words of thanksgiving to God?

"How much have you given me since I finally packed off to school? Or rather, have you been receiving stipends that should put smiles on your faces? Haven't you wondered what has been happening to make all this possible, even though I told you I had secured a teaching appointment—on a part-time, not a full-time basis?

"Today, I am here at home. I have brought foodstuff that has never before, since the world began, come close to this house. Do you still believe that my teaching appointment is footing the bills?"

"Have you joined a bad gang, my son? I could never imagine that. Oh my God," his mother cried.

"Don't talk like that. It is very harsh. And you know that Ucheaka could not be persuaded to do such a thing. He never stooped to such things, even do it when the prospects for this family appeared totally bleak and insolvably hopeless. How could you imagine that he would try such things now that he has succeeded in enrolling in a higher education program with prospects for getting better a job in the near future—a job that would ensure us a half bail from the life of penury?

"My son, we know very well that you are trying to care for us even though you're in school. Of course, you are a well-groomed child who is very conscious of our condition. But that is not the issue we are discussing here," Mazi Obilo said.

"What is the issue we are discussing here now? Just tell me! The issue is that I have come back in a different way—one that is much greater than our expectation. And instead of appreciating me and thanking God, you are here quizzing me on issues we should easily resolve, as if I have committed a crime," Ucheaka retorted, almost flaring up.

"Anyway, I must say that I anticipated this meeting, though not in this loathsome way. Should I be given this cold mournful welcome because I brought a blind girl home? That girl, you see, is my life, my god," Ucheaka said.

"Tufiakwa! You speak abomination. Don't say this again," Mazi Obilo warned his son, reeling in disappointment.

"Well, I shall take everything as coming from ignorance. If I were in your shoes, I think I may act similarly to this but with a more rational approach. Like I said before Father interrupted me with his 'tufiakwa,' that girl you see in that repulsive hut you call a house is the genesis, the nucleus of all these hidden and observable changes and hope you see now today—even that stipend I have been sending you.

"Father, Mother, I decided not to tell you till today because I wanted to know your reactions. I met her on the third day at school, after I had completely lost hope. My next decision was about to be to return home and call the school issues quits. I didn't even have a kobo remaining on me when I met her, apart from the transport fare that would have brought me back home.

"But the moment I met her, after feeling disinterested in her as you do now, I had my path opened up before me, never to close again."

"Amen!" his parents chorused, their mouths open in amazement, though not with acceptance of the girl.

"The very moment we met, I saw light for the first time in twenty years and ate a good food for the first time and felt like a human being, not the animal I had felt like before, for the first time. I felt a sensation previously unknown—I felt unusually great. I began to see the rays of hope and survival and started seeing the picture of this condemned house, praise to the high heavens, as it is today. Papa, Mama, that girl you see seated in there is my life, my luck, and my second Jesus Christ. It is to her that my luck is tied; it is to her that my success is tied. And if she were to separate from me, I would revert to being the mocked Ucheakachukwu, son of dehumanized, degraded, isolated, and damned Obilo. She is my luck, the nucleus of my life, and the happiness that can only be found in the success enriching us now, never to retreat again. I am speaking of the success we have arrested and kept under our control as a slave to hear and obey us."

"How do you talk like this, my son? Are you induced by some force? Are you really all right, Ucheaka!?"

"No, I am not in any way induced. I am perfectly all right. In fact, with Adanne and, as it happens, because of her issue, I am doing better than ever."

"Are you drunk, boy?" his father thundered.

Ucheaka's temper flared, but he remembered that he had behaved the same when Adanne had first gripped him. Thus, he absolved his people and calmed down, taking a short pause while breathing quickly.

"My son, we don't mean to attack you. Just understand our feelings. How will people see us, the jeered, adding another pinch of salt into the unending jeers?" his mother said slowly, while sobbing mildly.

"You are not wrong in your imaginations and assumptions. Of course, the hardships of poverty have deeply and adversely affected us. Hence, you can hardly understand. Papa, Mama, your eyes have not changed along with my new looks, because your hearts haven't changed. You still see me as the impoverished Ucheaka Obilo, but I am no longer that person. And neither are you two, which is something you must also understand, though I can feel your ignorance.

"As soon as we are through today, builders shall be working here in this compound tomorrow."

"Where ... Are you hypnotized? Why talk like this, son? You are only frightening us. You are the one making things muddy here. You are creating much fear in our hearts with your words," his father said, almost shivering.

"Mother, Father, I stop talking here. I shall say the rest in front of Adanne, my better half. I can't do anything in her absence anymore; that would be a big betrayal. I only obliged you because it is normal that we should talk in privacy first, so that you will know how to relate to the angel. Otherwise, I don't do anything in her absence, lest I betray my angel of life.

"You should follow me. In her presence, I will make my pronouncement. In fact, I will make my position known, and I will decide whether to leave and head back to the campus immediately or stay as I have come to do."

"Oh! I said it. Uche is sick. He has been charmed," his mother cried passionately.

"I am not sick, Mama. If was sick, I wouldn't know the direction to this place, and even if I knew it, I wouldn't come with a cab, unaided by neighbors over there. I am sound, sounder in mentality and physical well-being than ever. So don't imagine the impossible, Mother."

"But the family name, Ucheaka, the reputation," his father said.

Ucheaka burst into a hysterical laughter. He clapped his hands as he went to hold his father and mother together. They mildly resisted. "What name, Papa?" He laughed again. "If there is anyone sick here, it is you two. My apologies, but I must say the truth. You only make me laugh foolishly.

"What name and what reputation do you speak of, Papa? Does this family have a name other than *sorry*, a reputation other than mockery? You should say *repugnancy* or *repulsion*, rather than reputation. Reputation belongs to humans, not animals like us. Does this family have worth? What name has it ever had that is not a derogatory one, one that is not used for humans but better suited for animals? Have you ever been called an upstanding name before by anybody in this village? Have you in fact been thought of as anything better than a dog that feeds on feces? And to make it worse, you have been called all this with impunity because you cannot even complain, to say nothing of striking back against those who beat you. How many times have you been slapped without provocation, simply because your oppressor wants to beat somebody and comes to look for you to satisfy his longing? How many times have you finished working for somebody and he straight-out refuses to pay you in full as agreed and you have to pretend you are not offended or risk receiving a beating on top of the short pay? Did you dare ask for the money again at risk of attracting the general beating of the village? How many times were you pushed to the igwe for village debt, even as you have mortgaged everything you had and come back with bruises?

"Mother, how many times have our creditors seized our working implements, even as our land is on mortgage, without us coming even close to collecting the fruits we need? How many times were you chased out of the women's meeting for smelling or wearing only one wrapper, despite the fact that it was washed and clean?

"How many times have you been stripped naked for not wearing the women's uniform? And if you stay back for not having the uniform, they come to the farm to carry you, in fact push you there to use you as a caricature to ridicule? In all these times, we could only cry and console ourselves, healing our bruises with herbs. Papa, Mama, that life, those disgusting, hazardous, and absurd conditions are over from now on—never, never to return. Rejoice with me, your son. God has smiled upon us.

"Who is responsible for all of this? None other than Adanne, who is sitting in that disgusting room on a coconut shelf. She is the god of this redemption, the god of this bailment, the god of the unimaginable new lease on life we have today. If you like, follow me. If you don't, remain here. But following me means that we will talk in front of Adanne to solve all these riddles," Ucheaka said.

With that, he left his parents dumbfounded and motioning in different directions like brainwashed fools. They did not immediately understand what was going on, as their minds contemplated what stand to take.

They reasoned within themselves. Could this boy be serious? Could he be under some influence? No! Their son had never acted like this. He had never been this disrespectful. No, this was not disrespect, their minds challenged. He was trying to prove a point, a point of absolute truth. If Ucheaka was not serious, he couldn't walk out on them. *Ucheaka is our boy,* each thought, *with whom we have struggle in the enclave of injurious living and poverty. He can't just forget who we are, now that luck has shone on us. He must be serious; he must not be pretending.*

The mere mention of luck as they meditated quickened Uche's parents to self-consciousness. They remembered that he had said his luck was in the girl. They feel a bit relieved. Another mind opposed that, saying, *What luck? In a blind girl? Can any kind of luck be associated with a blind girl, whose life is locked up in everlasting hopelessness?*

No, he is only being smart, they each decided. He was just saying that as means to get them to believe his antics. But it couldn't work. They decided to go and hear the girl out. But immediately they reminisced about a sad and unspeakable scenario that happened to them. The parents had snorted sorrowfully, saying that, no matter what happened, even if a leper came to rescue the family from this handicap of life called poverty, they would accept it. Nevertheless the Obilos knew that those who were afraid of their position—of their possibly contagious poverty—did not associate with them and would rather refrain from seeing the unexpected changes than launch further attack. The Obilo family had suffered more than the worst criminals, even without committing any crime, other than being poor—a state they had not asked for and one that joined in shaping them into the people they were by usurping their properties.

As they stood memorizing Ucheaka's narration of their life's condition and consider the sheer possibility of change through the association of the blind girl, their children came to meet them. They told their parents that the girl was a very good girl, adding that she wasn't even fully blind, but saw a little with her glasses. She had asked whether they went to school and, upon hearing that they did not, she had been assuring them that they would return to school. They actually had resumed their school since Ucheaka had been sending the stipend. But they had deliberately told her that they didn't go to school, in order to see her reaction.

They had also told the girl that they helped their parents do farmwork for people. She had exclaimed, assuring them that the era of such degradation was over. She had said that they would not even go to those people's farms again, much less work for anybody else. If they liked farm work, she had told them, people would work their farm for them, just as they had worked for other people. She'd said that they should rejoice and be thankful to God. She had also advised them to forgive their oppressors and never bear grudges or harbor malice, as God was only testing their faith.

"She said all this?" the parents asked, astonished.

"Yes Mama, Papa. Come, let's go and greet her and thank her. They have brought a lot for us, Mama. You would not believe, Papa, how our lives have changed through this girl."

"Do you mean this, Chika?"

"Yes, Mama."

"In that case, let us go."

They left immediately entered the only room of the hut, where Adanne was sitting comfortably without a trace of worry. Her beautiful face beamed with a radiance that no one would see without cursing the devil for denting it with blindness. Her beauty alone was enough to win anybody's sympathy and ire against the devil's incursion on her face.

Her confidence was built on the hope that, whatever resistance Ucheaka's parents may come up with, Ucheaka was equal to the task and would, without haste, surmount it. Of course, their reaction was not unexpected. That was why Uche and Ada had not overreacted and had, instead, understood their worry as coming from their ignorance; they did not know how their present enviable status had come to be.

Of course, she knew that they couldn't succeed in persuading Ucheaka to succumb to them. Besides, it was crystal clear that they would understand and accept the situation with absolute sincerity when well tutored on how the events had led to the present moment had transpired. And any rate, if Ucheaka were to succumb, both would lose; Chief Otieke would never accept Ucheaka without Adanne. However, he would accept Adanne without Ucheaka.

As the Obilos entered the house, they saw an angel sitting in their room, which was lowly and awful. The hut's roof leaked, causing the perpetual irritation of a wet floor. Yet Adanne looked relaxed, as if she were in a palatial abode. This caused a degree of awe in the Obilos.

The Obilos greeted Adanne warmly and stood in enraptured disbelief waiting to hear Ucheaka's account of Adanne's personality and the circumstances leading to their meeting and unbreakable union. He had already given them a clue while the three of them were outside. But Uche's parents did not really understand this; their understanding was clouded by sentimental emotions that fuelled only a desire for Adanne to get out of his life.

"When a feeling becomes so passionate, it erodes the knowledge of other things". The intense feeling of hatred the Obilos had for Adanne on first sight (not because they had previously had an issue with her but because of her circumstantial predicament) made them go blind themselves. They could not see the sparkling black beauty she possessed or her humility and gentleness. Though the latter two aren't easily seen on a person's countenance, these qualities were conspicuous in Adanne.

Ucheaka began to narrate everything that had brought him and Adanne together. He wanted to detail how those circumstances had led to the outpouring of uncommon blessings that had broken the jinx of poverty—the occupation and resolute residence of the family.

"Mama, Papa, my brother and sisters, this girl you see here, this angel you see sitting beside me here," he said, sobbing with sobriety and clearing his eyes. Adanne too felt laden with his emotions and joined him as she tried to soothe him.

"What is this, Ucheaka? Stop this now and tell us your story. You are making us blush," his father cautioned him.

The lastborn, Chika, who had been holding Adanne as she sat in between them, touched him and said, "Brother, sorry!" And everybody laughed.

"Papa, Mama, this angel you see here, is where my luck, the luck of the family has been hidden or, better still, tied, all these years of abject poverty."

His mother, Chigere, went to hold him. She told him to stop crying and tell them what he had come to say. She added that, even though his story might be pathetic, he must be man enough to hold himself together.

"Papa, Mama, do you know what causes me to be so emotionally laden? It is that God visited upon me a hard separate unraveling or unfolding of my luck as tied to or hidden in this angel. It was a large and very passionate trial. I almost pushed this my luck away, in the exact same way you people reacted this morning. I, too, am guilty of that. Hence, I have tolerated your ignorance. In fact, I owe her my life for not allowing me to push her away. Instead, she held me in order to give me what God had given us as deposited in her.

"Despite my threats, she held me tightly, forming a bond that could not be broken. Ada, please forgive us." He sobbed again.

She too was crying. But she consoled him, telling him that it was over and shouldn't be brought up.

Meanwhile his parents were filled with anxiety, wondering what had actually happened. They pleaded with Ucheaka to release them from suspense and break the news.

"Papa, Mama, I didn't do rituals. Of course, you people know me. You trained me, instilling in me the fear of touching anything that would hurt me, as I have no one to defend me."

"Of course, we could swear on your behalf in your absence if you were accused of stealing. We know you, son. We would never think anything like that. Please don't go there," Obilo pleaded.

"Papa, I worked little and made huge riches. I am a bit rich now, as God has blessed us. I was not joking when I said builders will work here tomorrow. I have been favoured through this angel. I only decided to keep the news secret until the source of the blessing, the vault where the blessings were kept was here, bodily present.

"This blind girl, as you refer her, though she is not. She is my life, my living, my love, and the only source of happiness I have in my life. The happiness that escaped me for over twenty years visited and remained in me, the very moment I met and united with this angel of my life.

"She is the one through whom I have seen the stars the sun and the moon shine in my life. Before her, I saw and experienced only fire. You people are also victims of such circumstances." He sobbed.

"Oh! I have told you to stop this. You are nullifying this interesting story," his mother advised.

"Okay, I will not sob again. Just listen and hear me now. Papa, Mama, I never knew that my luck had been kept hidden in this blind girl. I never knew that Adanne was the source of my life, the spring water that supplied health to my living. Our transformation; our turning point for good; our answer to long supplications that seemed without answer; our joy and happiness, which we found elusive, was in a very close corner, a very close village."

He then narrated the story in full, right from the very hour he had left the hut for school. He told his family of the challenges that had been his companions. And he explained how those challenges had instantly given way to inroads to success right from the time he had managed (in fact been forced) to accept Adanne. He recalled her grip on him—all to bring about the success story they shared—and how she had refused to leave him, despite threats from the onlookers and even himself.

He explained the inexplicable sensation he'd had while leading Ada out of the registration arena and how they had sat down beside the school gate and talked, him feeling like someone in another world. He told them about the restaurant where they had eaten—his first experience of empathy from a fellow human being, who had bought him food when he had nothing left.

He described leading Adanne to the balcony, where he sneaked in to squat. That balcony, he told them, belonged to a former devil's agent, whose life was transformed by Adanne's ordinary, angelic, and spiritual statement, which had ultimately transformed all their lives. The statement, packaged in heaven, had changed the course of everything in their lives, he told them. It had given them not only life but also hope that would compensate for the century of poverty and insult that had ruled their lineage like inseparable twins.

Before Ucheaka could finish his statement, his mother fled to Adanne and held her firmly, crying profusely. She was overwhelmed with emotions because of the prospect of their family's departure from poverty in this life (and not just a slight or temporary departure, it seemed, but a permanent separation). And she cried because they had tried to reject the source of their changed life story, just as Ucheaka had almost done.

As Chigere held Adanne, crying, the rest of the family joined, all kneeling before Adanne and pleading for forgiveness.

Ada merely resisted their apologetic approach, threatening to leave the room if they didn't get up. They refused to be deterred by her threats. And so Adanne held them together, and they cried in chorus.

"That's enough. Let me finish," Ucheaka finally said, crying along with his family and the woman he loved.

They stopped crying, though the occasional sob could be heard as he continued. Now he shared Adanne's own emotionally writhing story. He told of the attack of the snake that had changed her beautiful life and left a mark that showed on her face today.

The account stirred in Uche's family a chilling sensation, throwing the entire room into a wail of dirges. All lost control as they rolled over themselves in sympathy with the beauty, the queen, the angel of the house of Mazi Obilo. Her story of sudden change would not be believed by the villagers, who feasted on the Obilo family as their outlet for mockery.

"Papa, Mama," Ucheaka called and paused again. He was temporarily at a loss for words, as he was chilled and thrilled over the rousing welcome, acceptance, and feelings of empathy expressed by his family to the darling Adanne.

Ucheaka could not refrain from the impulse of joy and ordered drinks. His siblings ran out immediately to get the drinks. The villagers who saw them were filled with bewilderment. It was the first time anyone had seen the Obilo Family buy drinks. None of them, however, spoke their usual taunting words, as they were all at a loss to explain what may have prompted this unusual occurrence.

When Uche's siblings returned, the celebration raged on like wildfire. The family could hardly utter words anymore, as their mouths were filled with biscuits and other treats Ucheaka had brought home. They only nodded their heads as they mobbed Adanne on her seat, cuddling and fondling her as if she were a precious baby.

Ucheaka stood up, beaming with a furious smile that could reveal the secret in his mind. He pointed to Adanne. "My people," he said, pausing to allow an unstoppable smile spread across his face. "My people, seated here is Ada, my life, my eternity, my glory. In fact, my luck has been in this blind girl here. We celebrate today here. We feel different now. No longer will we drown in worry. Rather, we will be buoyed the glut of comfort and unending joy. We will remain afloat in the life of goodness that the Lord God has kept inside this angel for the Obilo family for ages and generations past.

"My people." He stooped low and picked up Adanne like a baby

"Don't let your joy hurt me!" she shouted joyously.

As he carried Adanne in his arms, he thundered joyously. "Here we are today, celebrating. And we shall continue to do so from here on out—thanks be to my luck. We are here today, now and for ever, celebrating 'my luck in the blind girl.'"

All in the family caught up with the fire of Uche's appreciation, and the house was soon aglow with shouts of joy and merriment. "Our luck in the blind girl. Oh Lord, our Lord. Our Luck, our joy, our happiness, our lives as humans in the blind girl!" they chorused with enthusiastic, intoxicated joy as Ucheaka carried Adanne, spinning in a frenzy of joy in the small hut until both fell down gently on the rough red sand floor.

"Don't injure her, Ucheaka."

"Even if she gets injured now, it doesn't take away anything but brings in something."

The celebrations thundered on, unquenchable, leaving the mocking villagers who overheard them in absolute confusion. What could be going on in there? The villagers were absolutely perplexed. To them, the sounds coming from the Obilo hut didn't sound like sounds of sorrow but those of joy. The small children rushed down the road to peep, still careful not to enter the Obilo family's place; they did not want to be infested with the perennial disease of excruciating poverty.

The following day, as the celebration still raged like a wildfire denying everybody sleep, the Obilos, who still remained aglow, got ready for a journey to Adanne's home in the neighboring village. Hers was bounded by the next village that fell within their Local Council Area.

The intoxication of joy raves much more than the sadness of a heavy heart. The Obilos all got up from the vigil they had kept through the night. Joy drove the feeling of sleepiness away. This did not bother them, as they almost consciously kept vigil to make sure the unconfirmed Grace of God did not abscond in the night—just as it is said that somebody beaten mercilessly by a swarm of bees runs when he sees ordinary flies.

As the night gave way to morning, even though the intoxication of the drunken joy still hung over them, they prepared in earnest to make the journey. Ucheaka and his father had already made arrangements for the sand suppliers to start bringing sand to the compound, as well as for the arrival of the cement sellers. They arranged for builders, some of whom were from the same village and who came with their faces covered in shame.

Initially, they had been reluctant to come. They felt overwhelming shame, given the jeers and derision they had routinely thrown at the family. However, they remembered the incredible news of the sudden change of situation in the wretched lives of the

Obilos. Moreover, no other jobs were available. Some of the builders hadn't had any work for weeks. Hence, they unwillingly agreed to go, summoning up the spirit to resist the beatings of the invisible but powerful shame.

They wouldn't have agreed to this unimagined development if not for the undiluted reports of those children who had initially stood at a distance to peep but had later been lured in by the unresisting pressure of the presence of the uncommon biscuits and drinks Uche's siblings were enjoying.

Some of the builders did not come, not because they had others jobs to do but because they couldn't withstand the shame and its taunting. Thus, they denied themselves the opportunity to share in the uncommon grace God had bestowed upon the Obilos, who had been made into caricatures in the village. They lost the opportunity for a job after weeks of idleness because of self-judgment and self-condemnation.

Before the arrival of the builders (who would ultimately go back to give a concise report of the awesome happenings at Mazi Obilo's house), the villagers were in absolute chagrin as they saw big tippers passing along the road into the compound. Sand was then tipped around the compound onto uncleared bush; nobody had previously had the chance to do the clearing.

Joining the tippers was a lorry loaded with cement that was also offloaded in the compound, which had no roof other that the one covering the hut. It was not a very rainy period. Even if it was, Ucheaka's financial circumstance could tolerate the rain damaging the cement. Thank God, it did not come to that.

Some villagers still felt sure this phenomenon was a dream, doubting its reality as they self-consciously peeped through the holes in their fences to confirm what was happening at wretched Mazi Obilo's house. Their dream turned to reality when those builders from the village met them at the joints in the evening, wearing dumbfounded states as they confirmed the truth of what was happening once they could no longer remain mute.

And the village, the entire village, fell into an enraptured coldness. No one, save those who'd broken through their shame to go to work for the family, had the mind to go to Mazi Obilo's compound. They couldn't help but pass nearby by accident, though, allowing their eyes to catch them up with what was happening for the Obilos.

Those who worked on the compound worked like perfect slaves, following the stern warnings and conditions they had always meted out to Mazi Obilo's family.

The Obilo's neither took notice of them nor tried to retaliate. They only busily prepared for their departure to Adanne's house. Her family lived in the neighboring village after the sister village Umunkere of the same Local Council Area. Even if they'd had time to oversee the workers or stay with them on that day, they wouldn't have displayed any manner of repressive attitude. They wouldn't have attempted to repay the untoward and heinous maltreatment they had previously received, as though they were not known to God and vulnerable and attackable without regret.

The arrangements for the building work had partly been made during the previous evening's crazy celebration by Ucheaka; his father; and Ucheaka's immediate younger sibling, Onyemaechi. Onyema, though, had dropped back, at one point, reluctant to miss the inferno of wild celebration among his family, and Mazi Obilo and Ucheaka had continued.

The workmen settled down with their work, having been given enough money to eat by Ucheaka, since the family was going out and couldn't cook for them. They highly appreciated the allowance. The cabman who had brought Ucheaka and Adanne the previous day arrived, just as the couple had arranged. The family boarded the cab one by one and settled in for the journey to Adanne's home. Though the car was a station wagon, they squeezed in tightly and fit only with a bit of discomfort, as nobody wanted to be left behind. After all, save Ucheaka and Adanne, this would be, for all, their first journey in a vehicle.

At Adanne's house, the same scenario of amazement played out, almost as if the family had been electrocuted. Of course, the scenario was even more electrifying here than had been in Uche's house. Uche's family, after all, had a glimpse of hope for his success.

But when it came to Adanne, her family, especially her father, had seen her going to school as a foregone waste of time.

Adanne's family, too, stand in awe and bewilderment of all that was happening and tried to think fast and wake up from their slumber.

The scene was, in many ways, a repeat of the disbelief that had taken over Ucheaka's house, with one notable exception. When it came to the proposal of Ucheaka, the couple did not receive the slightest of objections. No sensible person with his or her full sanity intact would say no to such an astounding and handsome young man with full and complete physical aptitude. And here he was proposing to the disabled Adanne of all people.

Bemoaning all sadness of the past, without eliciting the travails that made up the present, Adanne and Ucheaka concisely and without mincing words narrated their meeting; the union; and, finally, the mission God had attached to it, bringing them up to where they were today. Their narration stirred another round of sober expressions; the Mazi Udenwa family sat with mouths wide open, listening without understanding, as their brains had been locked out by the shock of disbelief.

They were engrossed in disbelief. The story seemed like an exaggerated folktale. And Ada's family only moped like hypnotized people.

Nwayimma, who had been holding Adanne, along with Ada's siblings, cried but did not have the strength to fully demonstrate their emotions. The little strength they had after coming from the farm was sapped by this heart-blowing, incredible story. Adanne kept telling her family to stay with them and assuring them that the story was not a farce but a true happening, at least judging from her physical appearance, which captivated every man.

Mazi Udenwa, in a state of disbelief, roared again. "You people have come with these ideas of yours to cause me discomfort again." He didn't realize that he had said this because he was wrestling mentally, trying to capture what was going on.

Adanne admonished him to try to give way to the true condition of the present and let go of his poverty-entrenched life of doubts about life's dynamism.

With this statement, Mazi regained himself and shouted thunderously, "Is this happening? Am I dreaming or being deceived?"

"Yes, it is, Papa, and shall remain," Ucheaka replied, going to hold him down in his chair as he continue their story.

Uche also announced that builders would start work in the compound tomorrow, as they were very busy working in his family's house in Umuagwara village now.

This reverted Mazi Udenwa to mental comatose, for what he was hearing was impossible. The family burst into tears, joined by the Obilos. Nobody stopped anyone else, as everybody only tried to manage his or her own emotions.

Only Mazi Udenwa could be heard, shouting, "Ada, *gbagharam*" (Ada, forgive me)! He went to hold Adanne for the first time since the incident and felt as if he were touching the spirit. "Ada, gbagharam. I was only controlled by fear of the ravaging poverty, as the poor do not know when good things have come because of fear of the cost."

With this sensation, he shouted in joking fashion, "My son, you have a spirit partner here in my daughter."

"Of course I know, Papa. You need not tell me," Ucheaka replied.

"My daughter." He snorted, paused, and then left her to go and sit down. He fixed his gaze on her as he tried to reminisce about all the event of Adanne's life that had led up to today.

"Papa, you have to make arrangement for the builders for tomorrow. My father and I used the whole night to do ours," Ucheaka said.

"Should I start now? I am going already," Mazi Udenwa enthusiastically joked, standing up and pretending to go.

But Ucheaka met him to hold him back. "No, Papa, not now. When we are through with this ceremony," Ucheaka joked.

Adanne announced her decision to go with two of her siblings, particularly Nnachi. Ucheaka had earlier announced that they would go and start school again.

Her siblings jumped to their feet, filled with jubilation. The youngest one frowned furiously. But Adanne assured her that she too would come after they had finished the arrangements, and she cheered up again.

The fun extended into the town, with the unbelievable news spreading quickly. The villagers started arriving to see for themselves and greet the blind girl who had made the village proud.

Belief reverberated again when the villagers heard about all that had led to her return to school and eventually it to her attending the polytechnic. They praised her uncommon courage. She had not allowed physical disability to deter her spiritual ability, which like a car's piston kept firing so that it was finally given the chance to manifest itself.

Ucheaka ordered the boys to bring out assorted drinks they had bought on the way. Mazi Udenwa begged one of the palm wine tappers to go and tap his palm tree immediately, saying he would purchase the palm wine at a double price. The man replied that he had not yet sold his wine. He was about to go to the market before hearing the news and rushed down to see for himself.

Another one said that, even though another man had asked him to keep his wine for the day, he would go and bring it to Mazi Udenwa, who highly appreciated the gesture.

The unscheduled occasion took off, with people trooping in from all directions. Everybody had something to drink, as assorted drinks, including the palm wine, were available.

The celebration thrived, the uncommon merriment holding sway over all. People drank, especially the beers and malts that were only occasionally drunk and that had not been enjoyed for a long time. And everybody felt ecstatic.

Mazi Udenwa busied himself with drinks as he moved around chanting, "Drink. Be merry with me, as the Lord has remembered His own. Thank Ada for me."

The celebration continued with high spirits. The Obilos and Udenwas sat together at one side watching the event with due admiration, while Mazi Udenwa kept moving through the crowd in an unusual display of joy. Everybody felt high, even though they also felt sorrow over Adanne's condition. The jewel of the village had been disfigured.

Adanne herself did not feel similarly perturbed by her condition. She wrapped herself in the arms of Ucheaka, causing some awe in the minds of the people, who wondered what this handsome boy saw in the blind girl, even if she was beautiful.

Their deepest surprise came from the fact that the boy seems to be quite well off financially. Yet he had an unending interest in the girl.

Of course, the feeling of awe was not unexpected, as the people of the village were quite ignorant of the whole story. They only felt what they saw, without being privy to the real story. And they felt this despite the fact that, without Adanne's disability, no man would resist the sparkling black beauty. And they assumed that would matter to a man like Ucheaka.

The joy increased, and the pace of the occasion itself grew more rapid. Most strikingly surprising, Mazi Udenwa shouted, "Wait! Just wait!"

Everybody's attention turned to him to see what would come next and to ascertain why he would try to stop the occasion. Some villagers felt a cold of fear. Perhaps Udenwa had remembered some of the maltreatments they had meted out against him.

"Just wait! Wait I said," Udenwa said, staggering from the effects of the alcohol. He paused and stood in one place, though his footing wasn't strong. "Ada! I don't know what is going on here. Did you just bring drinks for us to drink? Oh! You just came to buy us drinks, knowing that we need this so desperately? Or did you come with a message?" Mazi Udenwa was hinting that he wanted the marriage rites to start immediately.

"But I don't understand, Papa. What do you mean? Are you not thrilled by the opulent joy that has filled everybody's hearts?" Adanne asked.

"But! Is he—" Uche cut in.

But before his son could say more, Mazi Obilo cut in himself. "Ucheakachukwu, the son of his father, sit down. You people are but children. I understand my friend very well."

"Okay, Papa. But what do you understand now?" Ucheaka asked.

"I have told you that you won't understand. Just watch us in parables," his father replied.

"Okay! You win, Papa. Old people and proverbs. We are curiously watching and listening," Uche told his father. He pulled Adanne close.

The people watched, drank, and made merry.

People saw the effects of booze evidenced in Mazi Udenwa's demonstration, but not in his last statement. It had a rational undertone.

"My in-law!" Mazi Obilo called, getting Mazi Udenwa's attention. "Oh!" he shouted clapping his hands jubilantly and dancing.

"Oh yes! He has delivered the message. He has said it. Aah! I was thinking you just came to buy us drinks to get merry. But you have now delivered the message. Ha ha!" Udenwa laughed.

The two wives sat together, jesting in a passionate mood. They giggled and jeered joyously at the men who like drinks. "Leave them. Men and drinks, they like this water of merriment so much," Nwayimma said.

"Especially as they've not seen even a drop to sip in a very long time. My fellow woman, my in-law, we can't thank God enough for these children He used to bail us from the quagmire of financial oppression," Ucheaka's mother replied.

"My in-law, I still don't believe what I see. I pray to wake up from this dream and find that it is still happening as reality. My in-law, only God can understand my feelings."

"Hmm! Yours is a dream that may turn true. Mine is a clear and consciously viewed simulation. I simply see it as a mimic of a great life displayed to entertain people. Everybody should revert to his or real life after the show." Ucheaka's mother said, snorting down sorrow.

"Even if they drink and fall on the ground today, even if they defecate on their own bodies, it is allowed. It would never raise any opposition. We can't simply believe this," Nwayimma, laughing and falling against Ucheaka's mother.

Together, the two women laughed hysterically, attracting joyful attention from the boozed crowd. They cracked jokes, danced, and mocked poverty—daring it to come to and display its fangs again, fangs that would never resurface. They celebrated and mocked their past years, in the presence of villagers who themselves were boozed and who joined them, dancing without steps, which were suppressed by outpourings of merriment.

"My in-law," Mazi Obilo continued. "My son saw a ripe *udara* fruit here in your compound—precisely, your family. Will you give us some? We are desperate, as no option remains.

"Mazi Obilo!" Mazi Udenwa exclaimed. "Me? In my house? Which house? It's your house here. By the way, there is no tree here. So where and how did you see the ripe udara fruit?" he added jokingly.

Everybody laughed and cracked jokes, saying, "Maybe it's this Akpaka tree that grew the udara tree."

"Of course, yes! My house is an Akpaka tree that would never grow udara fruit. But see today, a udara fruit, a ripe and beautiful one at that, is coming from it, which means that nothing is impossible in this life," Udenwa joked.

Everyone laughed again, accepting that the poverty-stricken Udenwa house was an Akpaka tree that had, today, grown the sought-after udara fruit. That house had, today, supplied merriment to the villagers, who never would have believed the possibility of such a strange occurrence. They all celebrated the powerful proverbial joke and danced even more fervently to the loud ovation, while drinks sought consumers.

"But if I may ask, is it the udara in your hands already, the one to be plucked, or the one on the ground yet to be picked up. You have the udara already. Just open it and share with us." He laughed as he joked and danced.

"Of course. It is in our hands but not ours until you give us the order to open it up and share with you. It is still yours, and that is undeniable. We wait only for your approval, as you are the only person who can give such an order," Mazi Obilo jokingly replied. He was trying to refrain from the impulsiveness of the influence of the alcohol. He wanted to show himself respect, even though nobody cared if anybody was under the influence of alcohol; the unexpected, unimaginable, and sumptuous joy of the day could tolerate that.

The merriment continued unabated. Everybody had taken his fill and showed it in his or her behavior now—except Ucheaka, Adanne, and their mothers and siblings. They only sat sipping their own drinks gently and watching the boozed entertaining themselves with the jokes and foolish laughter of drunken people.

Everybody felt satisfied and happy.

Suddenly, thunderous fierce shouting came from outside the compound. The sound was very frightening, like that made when one suddenly gives up the ghost. It didn't stop but increased in loudness, spreading anxiety to the crowd. Initially, it was the children who paid this cry heed. But soon they were joined by the adults, causing everyone to suspend the merriment, gain quick recovery from the possessiveness of alcohol's influence, and become fully alert to what was going on.

Mazi Udenwa's family, particularly Mazi himself, felt quite badly to receive such a slap in the middle of this first joy of life. And Mazi wondered who had chosen to die on such a day and at such an hour, to thwart what great merriment he had only seen once in his lifetime of over fifty years. He bemoaned the person, lashing out at him for not waiting till tomorrow. He felt utterly sorrowful as the shouts increased dramatically.

Mazi Obilo was wrapped in sadness. He wondered if his adversaries, who had never expected good things in his life, had followed him from Umuagwara village to Umuaku village to thwart his only happiness. He had, in fact, in this day found such great joy that he could give way to death after having it, if death so wished.

As the loud noise increased, circling the compound, the young men in their midst quickly rushed out to see what was disturbing their merriment. They were ready to beat whoever was involved if the disturbance thwarting the celebration turned out to be a frivolous one.

But as the young men rushed out, they met others (who had quite possibly been coming to Mazi Udenwa's compound on hearing the good news and that drinks were being lavished on guests there to share in it) chasing a very big cobra that had just emerged from the bush. They quickly joined in the chase, attempting to catch and kill it.

The influence of the alcohol gave them a very large boost, and the young men from the celebration outran the weaker ones who were already chasing it. The children who first saw what was happening started shouting helplessly. Adanne's experience had made the villagers, even the adults, fear and run from snakes, rather than going after them on spotting them.

Since Adanne had her experience some nine years ago, everybody feared even ordinary earthworms, to say nothing of going after a snake. Those who had attempted the chase before the boozed boys came out had only managed to summon the courage on the assumption that this might be the snake that had attacked Adanne. Catching it and hacking it down would surely score points with the family. Still, they chased it with caution and fear.

But when the boozed boys arrived, they chased after the snake without an iota of fear. The drinks they had consumed had driven away the possibility of fear in their eyes.

They pursued the snake relentlessly, not allowing it a chance to escape. It fled wisely, looking for a place to hide. It saw no good options, as the bushes near the compounds were not thick like those in the farmlands.

The boys refused to give up the chase. The cobra behaved as if it was putting them on, racing helter-skelter. It showed no sign of attempting to attack but only slithered for its dear life, especially as the boys were closing in on it.

The news of the cobra and the chase filtered into Mazi Udenwa's compound. More and more shouts of, "There it is! Over there!" could be heard.

Upon hearing of the news that the cobra was once again being pursued, Adanne instantly passed out. This created another round of tension in the compound. Everybody watched in suspense to determine her condition, and the compound was filled with ceaseless wailings.

Ucheaka cried, calling on God to please help him save his wife or take them both. Mazi Obilo soothed his son, telling him that Adanne had only passed out, that she would regain consciousness, and that it was just a response to shock.

Mazi Udenwa stood tall, dried-out, and senseless, only shouting, "Who wants to terminate my joy? Are you people not tired of ailing me? Have I not suffered enough!?"

Nwayimma, upon seeing her daughter pass out, passed out too, and the tension increased to a crescendo. No one knew who to attend to, Adanne or her mother. Meanwhile Ada's siblings only wailed, rolling on the ground while some elderly ones who hadn't followed the boys held them, soothing them.

Almost immediately, Adanne revived, and so did her mother. The pair joined in the crying. They held each other as Adanne recalled her suffering from the attack. Ucheaka soothed her, assuring her she would face no more problems and saying that God has answered them already. Nobody would thwart the presence of God in their lives ever again. That was already established.

She laid her head on his shoulder and enjoyed the sensation of his body touching hers. It soothed her emotionally, especially as she remembered that the official commencement of the marriage rites was in progress and the eating of the preciously awaited fruit was just a matter of hours away—though there was no room for privacy. Both families were living in huts in states that better suited a slum.

Simultaneously, Ucheaka was thinking the same, though along with his comfort, he was regretting the absence of privacy. He hoped that their parents would oblige and allow them to leave for their base in the polytechnic that evening.

Though this feeling of comfort in one another's presence renewed their joy, it was still suppressed by Adanne having passing out. In general, concern over her momentary unconsciousness was gradually dying down and the enthusiasm reviving, though it would never be as it had been before having been dented. Adanne and Ucheaka felt so emotionally aroused as they held each other that it was almost noticed by the other people, and they tried to dismiss the snake troubles.

But just as they earnestly tried to put the snake issue behind them, since Adanne had revived and they strongly desired to douse the troubles of their minds, behold they saw a sight they could not turn from. The boozed boys marched toward the compound carrying the frighteningly long cobra and scaring everybody.

The small boys fan behind their parents and other older people as the boozed boys walked along majestically, shouting songs of victory, dancing, and claiming that this was the snake that had attacked Adanne. They chanted war songs of victory, claiming that Adanne's problem was over. The Obilos looked on in suspense, while the villagers of Umuaku were happy and believed their claim. They trusted that their gods had shown mercy to the girl who had made the village proud.

The boys threw the cobra down on the ground and demanded a pot and yam immediately. Some had already started making a fire. Ucheaka only looked on without knowing what to believe, though he soothed Adanne, who had started crying again as soon as the boys arrived with the snake.

Mazi Udenwa rushed inside the kitchen to get the yam that his wife had been about to peel when the train of Mazi Obilo's family had arrived earlier in the day. He brought the yam and the pot and gave them to the boys. Some suggested cooking it as it was to save time, but the elders objected, saying that, since Adanne would eat the yam and drink the water, it should be peeled and cooked well enough for eating.

The boys cut the snake in parts and washed it immediately. They placed some of the parts in with the yam and started the cooking process, over-stoking the fire to make it cook quickly. They put nearly all the heaps of firewood Nwayimma kept into the fire, until it burned like a furnace, driving people away. The elders feared the boys would come to possible harm the way they were playing with the fire, which raged high like an inferno.

A few minutes led to almost an hour, and the boys pulled the yam dish from the fire, claiming that it had cooked, even though the elders advised them to cook it a bit more. In their hurry and curiosity and desire for Adanne to see again, they refused and ask for a plate.

One scooped the yam and the liquid from the pot onto a plate that looked like a plate children use for tea parties because of the family's poverty. Another demanded that Adanne come forward so he could wash her face with the water used in washing the snake.

The elders, though reluctantly, suggested that the chief priest be brought to perform the rituals. But the boys refused, querying as to the relevance of the chief priest, when he had not been able to do anything about the effect of the attack nine years earlier. The elders were not really forceful in their suggestion anyway, seeing the zeal and faith of the boys.

But just as Adanne went to step forward for the washing of her face, the chief priest appeared from the road and stopped the boy. "Hey!" he cried, still standing on the main road. "Stop!"

The elders feel were very happy that he had arrived.

The chief priest asked the boys on whose authority they were acting. This triggered the anger of the boys, who were ready to cast him out, saying he lacked both powerful and efficacy. But the elders calmed the situation.

The chief priest, who had seen that the boozed boys were ready to humiliate him, mellowed out by force and spoke peacefully. He praised the boys to high heaven, praying for prosperity for them.

He then made some incantations. So enrapturing were these incantations that everybody believed his presence actually mattered in that situation and that, without it, nothing would have worked. He even spoke of the appearance of the snake, which had been hidden by the gods for the fulfillment of what was taking place today. Everybody who was anxious to have him perform the ritual and let the pretty jewel see concurred.

The boys were convinced. But they were impatient with his long sermon. Even the elders understood, as they too felt they were being kept in suspense.

Mazi Obilo and Ucheaka only prayed in their minds, while Uche's mother recited the rosary inquisitively. Everybody was obsessed and in suspense. As the chief priest's marathon of incantations continued, impatience entered and enveloped the crowd.

The chief priest then ordered the boys to wash Adanne's face. The boys jostled for the privilege as Adanne stepped out. Then one of the boys washed her face, feeling some sensation as he touched her beautiful face.

Next, the chief priest ordered Adanne to eat the food prepared with the snake meat. In addition, he warned that nobody should eat the remaining part of the snake other than him. The boys protested—until Ucheaka promised to give them enough money for Nkwobi, Isi ewu, and pepper soup. Then they were happy to leave the snake meat to the chief priest.

Ever since Adanne's incident, the people of the village dreaded snakes, and they rarely ate snake meat, even when a snake was killed. This had not been the case in the past, when snake meat had been considered a very good meat that was denied nobody. Now, though, everybody hated it with passion. People sometimes killed snakes and left their carcasses on the road to decay and, ultimately, dematerialize.

Ucheaka carried the plate to feed Adanne. But one of the boys, agitated (though he spoke with a light and playful tone), said, "She is only your wife, but she is my sister. I shall feed her. Just step aside. When we finish, we will hand her over to you."

"Okay! I surrender," Ucheaka said playfully as he retreated.

The boy carried the plate to feed her.

The odor was very offensive, unlike the normal snake they used to eat. Even though the chief priest had mentioned it during his incantation, Adanne felt uncomfortable with the offensive odor. She closed her mouth as the food was brought close. Ucheaka held her, encouraging her and telling her that, if someone else could eat it for her, he wouldn't even allow her touch the plate but would eat it for her.

She kept pulling back, feeling resentful toward the odor and thereby extending the suspense. The boy kept pleading and petting her while Ucheaka caressed her, but she still dragged her feet. Both of her parents joined in, encouraging her, as did the elders.

Still Adanne resisted the food, and the boy forced it into her mouth. The moment her mouth touched the spoon and the water slipped past her lips, her eyes instantly opened, and she regained her sight. To the world out there, it would remain incredible but the tradition of the people had made the villagers believe in the possibility as it actually turned out to become.

She jumped to her feet, shouting uncontrollably, "I can see!"

She hugged Ucheaka and stared into his face. They held each other's gaze and then hugged, each gripping onto the other and crying. To them it would have been a lost union that would make each not feel the true goodness of the world, though the travails to the making of the union was quite escruciating. Nevertheless, the overwhelming joy of the union had surmounted it. And to be a good lesson to others to learn, even though Ucheaka was still visited with sense of guilt occasionally until it gradually fizzled out after Ada's unrelented consolation.

Ucheaka, who was beaten by disbelief, cried like a baby. Nobody noticed, as all were jumping in jubilation. Adanne held Ucheaka in her firm grip. She couldn't believe how handsome he was. She had only ever had a glimpse of the man she loved. Uche cast his mind back to Adanne's grip at the registration arena. He fell to the ground. Adanne was crying profusely.

Everyone watched on in amazement, interpreting the couple's reactions as simple happiness.

But for Uche it was not. Her grip reminded him of the grip he had wanted to push away—the grip that had groomed him and had given him life and the grip that was the ground upon which he stood today.

He cried and spoke loudly, so everyone could hear and understand why he cried, "God, you tested me with a blind girl. You bound my life, hid from me the possibilities, and sentenced my life to see if I would go for it. God, I can't claim to have passed. I failed because I wanted to push this girl away, but you made her grip on me strong, just as she is holding me now. God, how awesome you are. Today, I am rich with luck and in life. I and my future generations will be tied to the blind girl, who can now see and whose blindness was a test. Oh my life is in the blind girl; my luck is in the blind girl."

The atmosphere in Mazi Udenwa's house was so charged words are not sufficient to describe it. People came from far and near to see. Those selling drinks and food in the village and neighborhood emptied their shops for Uche Ada, even as they doubled their prices. He paid, even forfeiting his change.

The duo married officially. Their business triumphed. It finally grew into a conglomerate that supported all three families—Mazi Udenwa's, Mazi Obilo's and Chief Otieke's. Their children married and lived abroad, creating the next generation. The conglomerate spread across the nations, with chains managed by members of the three families, who were brought together through marriages and lived peacefully and happily as a family, a lineage, and a genealogy.

Uche and Ada lived with an attitude that they made sure every member of the three families imbibed—one of humility and thankfulness to God. They started a foundation called AdaUcheaka Foundation for the Development of the Forlorn (AFDF).

The duo lived not just in comfort but also in heaven. Adanne and Ucheaka weren't without each other for more than ten minutes, even to ease themselves.

In addition, they were the founders of a ministry for God called "Mission For Revealing Need For Unconditional Love". The ministry's theme came from the Book of Hebrews 13:1. It eventually developed into a church, where people were taught about why they should not discriminate in their service to God and man. Practitioners learned that they should be kind to everyone they saw on the roads. No one knew who might be an angel of God, as Adanne was to Ucheaka.

Ucheaka called Adanne "My Blind Girl." And Adanne called him "My Blind Boy"—on the grounds that he did not see beautiful girls but had hooked himself to a disabled girl.

About the author

Mazi Bonny Iyke Odiche Ozoma is a gifted and prolific writer. At the time of writing *My Luck in the Blind Girl*, he had been writing for over twenty years in the fields of fiction, Christian religion, and social arts.

He trained at Federal Polytechnic Oko Anambra, Nigeria, and hails from Umuaka Imo State in Nigeria. He is married with children. He is the leader of Christian Conscience Advocay(CHRISCAD), concerned for return to Christian primitive state.

He finds his topics drawing on inspirations and circumstances around him. Fondly called Odenkpisi by his admirers, his business is writing.

The phone number is: 07068385032 or 234 7068385032.
The email is: odiche33@yahoo.com.

About the book

Luck of the Blind Girl is about a girl from a remote village who was very keen on education. Gifted both mentally and physically, she became the love of the village. She was also honest, respectful, and devoted to her Christian faith.

Suddenly, her life became twisted when an incident left her blind. But in blindness, she did not give up her purpose. Her desire for education remained high. She struggled to get a pair of glasses to aid her sight and went back to school. Though she came from a wretched home, she was determined to be educated. The threatening poverty did not deter her, even though it affected her siblings.

In another town, there lived a boy in a similar financial circumstance. The poverty his family faced was even worse than hers. The boy was brilliant, so much so that his parents were ready to go naked just to see him through his education. Yet they lived in abject poverty, a state of life that made the rest of the village stigmatize them.

The boy and the girl met during a fraught registration process after each had received admission into a polytechnic. In a queue, the girl held the boy tightly so as not to lose her position. Even after the registration officers had closed their doors, she still gripped onto him, not knowing the registration windows had closed and, thereby, creating a scene. The boy wanted to push her aside, but she pleaded with him, promising him that her God would bless him. He tried to explain that the office had closed, but she refused to understand, as she could not see. The scene caught the registration officers' attention, and the officers surprised everyone by favoring the duo, giving rise to jealousy in the others.

The boy led the blind girl to the balcony of a wicked man, where he had been squatting unnoticed for two days. Suddenly they attracted the attention of the vicious man, who stormed out to harm them. But the girl spoke to him like an angel, and he felt the promise of new life. He was freed from the brutal life he had been living ever since his trusted friend had duped him. He accommodated the duo, to the surprise of his family, who had long dreaded and avoided him because of his wicked ways.

To compensate the pair for saving his life, the man opened a small shop for them in front of his house. That shop blossomed into a large business that bailed the two wretched families from a lifetime of penury. The families became sought after, rather than stigmatized for carrying the disease called poverty.

The business also helped their benefactor, who was a retiree, care for his own family. The three families lived large and were connected ever after.

And later, the girl regained her sight after marrying the boy.

www.ingramcontent.com/pod-product-compliance
Lightning Source LLC
Chambersburg PA
CBHW071852070526
44583CB00016B/1660